GOD OF ME

GOD OF ME

30-Day Devotional

NorthRoad Community Church Staff

Bold Vision Books
PO Box 2011
Friendswood, Texas 77549

Bible Versions listed on Page 189.

Table of Contents

A Word from Pastor Matt

Hey Church!

I am so excited that you have picked up this book and chosen to start a 3o-day journey to discover the God who is truly ruling and running your life. I know from firsthand experience that Satan is a master at walking into our lives and convincing us we need more than Jesus to thrive. It's that small lie that misdirects our hearts toward so many other things.

My challenge to you is, as you take this 3o-day devotional walk, to ask yourself hard questions, and make the determination to allow God to be the true God of you!

I love you all and can't wait to watch the transformation in so many of our lives.

~Matt Bartig

1

God of Me, An Introduction

Matt Bartig

As you read the title of this book, *God of Me*, you're probably thinking, *Wow, what a narcissistic name for a book. This guy thinks God was created for him.* At this point, you're probably ready to read it just to see how crazy one selfish man's thoughts can be. But hear me out.

We all have a God of us. God by definition is:

1. In Christianity and other monotheistic religions, the creator and ruler of the universe and source of all moral authority; the supreme being.

2. In certain other religions, a superhuman being or spirit worshiped as having power over nature or human fortunes; a deity.

As you read these definitions, I want you to focus on a couple of statements. "Ruler of the universe," and "power over human fortunes."

Think about that for a moment. Whatever is the god of me is, first, the ruler of my universe and, second, his rule will determine my fortunes (future).

Little g vs. Big G

Unfortunately, "gods with a little g" come in all shapes and sizes—a dream, a vice, a reputation, or a hobby, just to name a few.

It's these "little g gods" that can, if I'm not careful, become the ruler of my universe and will, in turn, determine my future.

Bara Dada, an Indian philosopher who lived in the 1920's, said, "Jesus is ideal and wonderful, but you Christians, you are not like him." He was describing a condition that is an epidemic among western society Christians. These Christians create "little g gods" to fit their lifestyles and reject the "big G" God who is real, who created them, and who wants to give them life.

Let's Look at Ourselves

How does it happen? How does a person go from a relationship with the big G God to a cheap counterfeit with a little g?

We're told in 2 Corinthians 13:5 that we should examine ourselves. "Examine yourselves, to see whether you are in the faith" (ESV). Daily we should take a long look in the mirror at who we are and who we are following. Ask ourselves hard questions and then make the conscious choice to follow.

Did you know the fear of mirrors is known as eisoptrophobia or catoptrophobia? Most people with this phobia are not actually afraid of the mirror itself. Rather, they are afraid of seeing what's within. They fear they won't like what they see, so they simply don't look.

I can so relate to this. I hate to look at my flaws. It's embarrassing. It represents failure. It proves I am not the person I truly want to be. If I don't look at it, then maybe I will somehow escape having to come to grips with my failures, and then I will be okay.

But That's Not Okay

This kind of thinking is the textbook work of the devil in our lives. In John 10:10, we're reminded that Satan is a thief. "The thief comes only to steal and kill and destroy" (ESV). He wants to steal your focus with little g distractions, kill your worship of the Big G God, and ultimately destroy your life.

If Satan can convince you that a cheap, counterfeit god is enough to give you happiness — even if it's momentary — and if he can pull your worship away from the true God, then he can nudge you in a direction that can altogether change your future.

When I was a kid, I remember watching *Snow White*. Do you remember the wicked queen? She was evil, but hey, she had the courage we need to win this battle. Each day she looked into the mirror and asked it if she was still beautiful. True, her style was absolutely narcissistic, but stick with me for a moment, because we can still learn a lot from her. Each day she checked her condition. That's not a bad idea. She was looking for outer beauty, but we should look for inner change.

What Will You See?

Try this on for size: *Mirror, mirror on the wall. Who am I choosing to allow to lead me? The God who first chose me? Or the one that I have chosen instead? Is my life really on purpose, or somewhere down the line have I changed my allegiance and lost my purpose altogether? Do I seek to do His will or my own?*

As you start this 30-day devotional, our goal is that you will see it as a kind of mirror. Each day you will come with us on a journey to contemplate this question:

Mirror, mirror on the wall who is God of me, after all?

Okay, I'm moving on from the Disney cliches. But seriously, we want to challenge you, really challenge you, to look hard into these stories before you and into your life, and to ask the hardest question you can ask: Is God truly the God of me?

This could be the most life-altering thing you will ever do. So go ahead. Look into the mirror and start the journey. I dare you.

2

This Is All About a Choice

Shawn Ohlms

"And Peter answered him, 'Lord, if it is you, command me to come to you on the water.' He said, 'Come.' So Peter got out of the boat and walked on the water and came to Jesus. But when he saw the wind, he was afraid, and beginning to sink he cried out, 'Lord, save me.' Jesus immediately reached out his hand and took hold of him, saying to him, 'O you of little faith, why did you doubt?' And when they got into the boat, the wind ceased. And those in the boat worshiped him, saying, 'Truly you are the Son of God'"

(Matthew 14:28-33 ESV).

What if I told you the God who called Peter to walk on water is the same God calling out to you in this moment? He is the same God who can do the miraculous in the midst of the mundane, and I believe He is calling each one of us to not only pursue Him with a fervent zeal like never before, but also asking us to choose calling over comfort.

Peter had two options. Like the other disciples, he could rest in the comfort of the boat. Or he could step out of comfort and into his calling, knowing that if he fell, he would fall one step closer to Christ.

Choose Calling Over Comfort

As we read in Matthew 14:28-33, Peter does the miraculous. He walks on water. When we dissect the passage, we understand Peter did this, not because he was anyone special, but because he understood who was calling him. When Peter said, "Lord, if it is you," he was using one of the four classes of "if" statements of conditions in the Greek language. When someone used this type of statement, it was a statement made with certainty. Peter was essentially saying, "Lord, *because* it is you, command me." Sometimes the only reason we need to say yes is that it's the Lord who is calling us. We don't need a multitude of reasons to say yes. We don't need to look for external signs. God's calling should be enough. No matter the circumstances. No matter the cost. No matter the hurdles.

Even in the midst of doing something incredible for God, we cannot be so naive to think the storms will stop raging. Notice the storm continued even while Peter walked on the water, and the moment he and Jesus returned to the boat, the storm ceased. It is essential to keep our focus on Him and not the storm. Peter was walking on water, sharing an incredibly intimate moment with the Lord, and still lost focus.

I have been there before. There is this emotional, eye-opening moment when everything finally makes sense. We walk away from that moment with a renewed zeal and seemingly greater purpose, only to be reminded of just how damaging life's storms can become. For Peter, this moment resulted in the miraculous (walking on water) becoming the predictable (sinking like a rock).

When we take our eyes off of Jesus, we become so easily distracted by everything the world throws at us that, in the blink of an eye, we begin sinking. It is in those moments we must, like Peter, call out to the Lord and, in complete humility, recognize it's only God's power working through us which allows us to experience the miraculous.

Why Do You Doubt?

As Peter stepped out of the boat, he exhibited un-adulterated confidence that the Lord would allow him to walk on the water. His journey away from comfort in pursuit of calling began with incredible passion and purpose. As the storm raged, however, that momentary zeal quickly dissipated.

Does this sound familiar to you? Have you started a journey like this before, only to be consumed with what's going on around you, and as you began to sink, fell back into complacency?

Peter realized the extent of that fall when Christ looked at Him, and said, "Why did you doubt?" Think about how simplistic that statement is. It was almost as if Christ looked at Peter, crouched down next to him as Peter coughed up water, and said, "Peter, buddy, did you forget everything I've done? Seriously, just last night, we had that whole loaves and fish moment. Bro, I know you're a fisherman, but you can't be that dense, can you?"

There will undoubtedly be moments throughout this journey when you hear the voice of doubt. We know that voice all too well. It will be the one telling you, "You're just too busy," "What can God do in only 3o days?" and "You've tried things like this in the past—how will this be any different?" In those moments, it is absolutely imperative to hit your knees and beg God to silence that voice. The reason Peter sank was not that the storms raged too strong. Nor was it because the waves crashed higher than God could handle. Peter became consumed with fear as his focus was diverted from God to the storm.

In our walk with Christ, fear and faith cannot exist as companions.

As we walk through the next 3o days, continually pray that as God cultivates a heart of change within you, your faith will be greater than your fear. When you sit in the *S.S. Comfort*, pray God will show you what your calling looks like and how to pursue it. As you journey through *God of Me*, will you commit to getting uncomfortable? Will you commit to taking big steps of faith in pursuit of looking more like Him? It's time for us to flee the comforts of complacency and begin pursuing a purpose like no other.

This is only day one, but if you will commit to completing this journey, you will not only experience remarkable changes, but you will also be able to look in the mirror and say with confidence, "God truly is the God of me."

Father, as we begin this journey, it is our prayer that You would call us to take big steps of faith. We ask You to make us uncomfortable. Lead us to step out of the boat of comfort, understanding that though we may sink momentarily, You will reach Your nail-scarred hands out to us and pull us from the depths of the water. God, as we seek after You, may we do so with the understanding that following You does not exclude us from the storms of life. When the storms rage, may we walk with confidence, knowing it is only when You are truly the God of us we walk without being overcome by the crashing waves around us. Lead us from comfort to calling. We pray this in the name of the one who is able. Amen.

3
This Is All About Love

Greg McGhee

"Let all that you do be done in love"

(1 Corinthians 16:14 ESV).

All those years as a kid asking folks, "How do you know when you've met *the one*?" Well, I knew when I met her. I knew it from the first date. Roxanne Jane Remole was going to one day be Roxanne Jane McGhee. The hard part was convincing her. So I began my quest to "get the girl." Spoiler alert: We've now been married for 20-plus years (time flies).

I remember the first time I told her I loved her. A buddy of mine had been asking me how "hooked" I was. He explained, "you know, when you're fishing, if you hook a fish with one hook, there's a chance he could get loose. If you hook him with two hooks, those chances go significantly down. If you hook a fish with three hooks, it's all over but the shoutin'." Then he glared at me and asked a simple question. "Greg, how many hooks does she have in ya?" I quickly and confidently replied, "Three!"

So when the time came, I went to him for advice, and we came up with a pretty crazy plan. I made her two of the same dish. I cooked one to the best of my ability. The other I intentionally made horrible. Where it called for sugar, I replaced it with salt. Yuck. Before I told her I loved her, I would serve her the nasty dish. *If she said she liked it, then she must love me.* Then I would know it was safe to confess my love for her. Well, as immature a plan as it was, it worked, and the rest, as they say, is history.

What Is Love, Really?

Love is an enigma, isn't it? You can't describe it. You can't look at it, taste it, or measure it. But love is one of the most used, abused, and misunderstood words in the English language. The Greek language had several words for love. Phileo (brotherly love), Eros (romantic love), Agape (unconditional love), among others. The word used in 1 Corinthians 16:14 is "Agape."

Agape is unconditional. It's a choice. A conscious decision of the will to put the needs and desires of another person above your own. Probably the closest example we have of that kind of love in our world today is the love of a parent for a child. Even though marital love should be on this same level, the divorce statistics would indicate it's not. But the parent/child relationship in our culture is still strong. It's not perfect. You still hear of parents who do things to their children nobody who truly loves another person would do. But overall, if you're a parent, you love your child, even when that child dirties a diaper, writes on the wall with a marker, flunks a class, misses the winning shot, or disobeys your wishes. We still *love them.* This is Agape. Love without conditions. I love you. Not "I love you, *but ...*"

What Is This?

What is the "this" in the title "This is All About Love?" This relationship. This life. This calling. This purpose. This church. This mission. It's all about love. Boil it down and cut the fat, and where you end up is love. The Apostle John in his books 1, 2, and 3 John makes this so clear. He says, "Anyone who does not love does not know God, because God is love" (1 John 4:8 ESV).

One of the biggest misunderstandings about love is the idea that it's a feeling. It is not. Love does produce a plethora of feelings. But love itself is not a feeling. Love is a choice. Often we follow our feelings wherever they take us. That can lead us on a crazy, turbulent ride. God has not called us to follow the whims of our feelings, but to make choices that honor Him. And when we do, feelings follow.

So who are you struggling to love? Your wife? Your children? Your parents? Your coworkers? Are you struggling to love God?

Well, here's what you can do with people. Love them practically. Bless them. Do things that people who love other people do. Think of them. Buy them their favorite candy. Send them an encouraging text. Above all, pray for them, and see how God turns your heart toward them.

It's similar with God. Love Him. Talk to Him. Spend time with Him. Honor Him. Worship Him. Sure, some of these may feel awkward at first, but over time your feelings will follow your choices.

Let's Love

There is much God has called us to do. The vast majority can be accomplished by mastering this one truth spelled out for us in Matthew 22:37-40. "And he said to him, 'You shall love the Lord your God with all your heart and with all your soul and with all your mind. This is the great and first commandment. And a second is like it: You shall love your neighbor as yourself. On these two commandments depend all the Law and the Prophets'" (ESV).

Love. When you don't feel like it, love. When they don't deserve it, love. When you're hurting, love. When you're grieving, love. When you're tired, love. After all, Jesus loved you first.

God, I am so grateful for Your love for me. I certainly don't deserve it. I have betrayed Your love and trust so many times, yet You love me anyway. I pray You would give us the strength to be like Christ in this way. That we would love the people in our lives anyway. I pray the prayer of Jesus, that all men would know that we belong to Him because we have love for one another. I love You, Jesus. Thank You for loving me first ... anyway.

4
You Chose Me

Richie Rhea

"You did not choose me, but I chose you"

(John 15:16 ESV).

No one would choose me, I thought. The awful part? I was right. I was the new kid on the fourth-grade playground. The two captains took turns picking people for their ball teams. I was the last one chosen. "Okay, come on, puny little new guy—probably a rotten ballplayer. Guess I'm stuck with you."

Most of us have had that experience. What a terrible feeling.

Something Very Different

But with the *God of Me*, something altogether different has happened. He chose me. And it had nothing to do with my ball-playing abilities. Or absolutely anything else I could do. It was because of His love. Paul wrote, "For we know, brothers loved by God, that he has chosen you" (1 Thessalonians 1:4 ESV).

Why do I need to know that God chose me? Because I need to know about His ultra-amazing love and grace. Knowing the love of God is empowering. And stabilizing. And removes arrogance. And so much more. The Bible talks about being "rooted and grounded in love" (Ephesians 3:17 ESV).

Understanding God's love gives me a richer understanding of just how God becomes the God of me. It is by His grace through Christ. He does it all. He gets all the credit. "So that no human being might boast in the presence of God" (1 Corinthians 1:29 ESV).

It's hard to imagine. The Greatest One chose me, the least. Go ahead and say right now to Jesus, "You chose me." Be amazed. Be humbled.

Who Did the Choosing First?

Most of the time we talk about how we chose Christ. Which is a great thing. But the Bible talks a lot about how Christ chose us. Jesus wants us to know, "You did not choose me, but I chose you" (John 15:16 ESV).

When it comes to my marriage, I used to think about how I chose Rhonda. I went after her. I asked her out.

Later I proposed. Down on one knee, the whole bit. But now, after over 40 years of marriage, I have a more realistic and accurate knowledge of my wife. Today, I realize she is even more loving and brilliant than I knew back then.

Did I choose her first? Or did she draw me in before I even knew what was happening?

There's a song by Randy Newman that pretty much expresses what I understand about those questions. The song is titled, "She Chose Me," and in it, Newman sings about how thankful he is that of all the people his girl could've chosen, she chose him. That's exactly how I feel. Except instead of just a generic thanks, I thank the Lord. And I thank my wife.

There's another song, a great old hymn, that says, "Oh, how I love Jesus, Oh, how I love Jesus, Oh, how I love Jesus, because He first loved me" (author of text, Frederick Whitfield [1824-1904], author of refrain, anonymous, Public Domain).

Know This Love Beyond Understanding

This is important to understand. Although, in some ways, I realize I don't understand it fully at all. God's love, like God's ways, is above me. I'm so glad God is way smarter than I am. I wouldn't want it any other way. "As the heavens are higher than the earth, so are my ways higher than your ways" (Isaiah 55:9 ESV).

Yes! He loves far more than we might imagine. Check out Ephesians 3:20–21. I feel so sorry for those who believe in a god who is no bigger than their own imagination and who is, therefore, no smarter or loving than they are.

What Does This Mean for You?

God chose you because of His love—not your looks or skills or anything else. You were "chosen by grace" (Romans 11:5 ESV). Amazing loving grace.

God chose you. You are forgiven. No charge will stick. Let this soak in. "Who shall bring any charge against God's chosen ones? It is God who justifies. Who is to condemn? Christ Jesus is the one who died—more than that, who was raised—who is at the right hand of God, who indeed is interceding for us" (Romans 8:33-34 ESV).

We are called to humility. No one will brag in heaven about self. "But God chose what is foolish in the world to shame the wise; God chose what is weak in the world to shame the strong; God chose what is low and despised in the world, even things that are not, to bring to nothing things that are, so that no human being might boast in the presence of God" (1 Corinthians 1:27–29 ESV).

The humble receipt of God's loving choice changes how you see others. He not only choose you by grace, He chose others too. Revelation 5:9 says of Jesus, "You were slain, and by your blood you ransomed people for God from every tribe and language and people and nation" (ESV).

We're Going to Make It!

Because of God's choosing, according to His love and grace, we can know we are going to make it. "He will send His angels with a loud trumpet and they will gather together His elect (God's chosen ones) from the four winds, from one end of the heavens to the other" (Matthew 24:31 AMP). And then justice will happen. "Will not God give justice to his chosen ones, who cry to him day and night?" (Luke 18:7 NIV).

Father, thank You for loving me. Thank You for loving me with a love that caused me to love You. Forgive me for doing so many really dumb things to convince someone to love me or to prove to myself that I'm worth loving, when all the while You loved me. You matter more. Your love matters more. Thank You for loving me with a love that reaches back beyond time and that will last for eternity. Help me comprehend Your love. Chase away my fears with Your love. Cause me to be rooted and grounded in Your love. Give me faith to trust Your love. All through Jesus. Amen.

5

And I Choose You

Melinda McDonald

"Today I have given you the choice between life and death, between blessings and curses. Now I call on heaven and earth to witness the choice you make. Oh, that you would choose life, so that you and your descendants might live! You can make this choice by loving the Lord your God, obeying him, and committing yourself firmly to him. This is the key to your life. And if you love and obey the Lord, you will live long in the land the Lord swore to give your ancestors Abraham, Isaac, and Jacob"

Deuteronomy 30:19-20 (NLT).

My niece and nephews were over the other day, and I found myself on the floor doing puzzles. I modeled, guided, and did most of the first puzzle for my nephew, trying to teach him how to work a puzzle. Do the outside first. Next, get colors or shapes together. Then the picture will be complete. He intently worked at that puzzle as I handed him the pieces and showed him where they belonged.

After completing the first puzzle together, he began a new one and said, "Me do it!" So I made sure all the pieces were there and sat back, watching him work to do the puzzle by himself. He was not using any of the strategies I had shown him. Instead, he was forcing pieces into places they didn't fit. He kept trying on his own, even walking away when he was frustrated.

As I saw his frustration, I asked if he would like my help. But he insisted, "Me do it!" So I sat watching and waiting as he abandoned one puzzle in frustration and started another. The next puzzle, too, became a jumbled mess, with the picture looking nothing like it was supposed to. I still sat, waiting for him to ask for my assistance. He had been clear he wanted to do it himself.

I was so relieved when he finally asked for help. Without doing it for him, I gave suggestions. He remained determined to do it. He took the puzzle pieces I suggested and soon saw a picture he could recognize. A firetruck. He was so excited.

Just one piece was left. Without it, the puzzle wasn't complete. My little nephew looked all around but couldn't find it. "Look behind you," I coached. He spotted it, grasped that last piece, and slid it into place. The picture was finished. He was so elated and had to show his dad as soon as he arrived. He pulled his dad toward the puzzle yelling, "Look, look, look!"

God, the Ultimate Puzzle-worker

Life can be like puzzle-solving, can't it? Only God can fill the spaces to make us complete. As we seek Him, He puts it all together to create a beautiful picture. He will not force Himself or His ways on us, but patiently waits for us to choose Him.

In Deuteronomy 30:19-20 (above), God spoke through Moses, challenging Israel to choose life and obey God so they could experience His blessings and live fruitful lives. He gives the same challenge to us. He never forces His will on us. God allows us to choose to come to Him and ask for His guidance. Ultimately, He lets us decide whether we will follow Him or reject His way. When we choose God, the puzzle makes sense and a beautiful picture is complete, a life picture He perfectly planned for us.

"God saved you by his grace when you believed. And you can't take credit for this; it is a gift from God. Salvation is not a reward for the good things we have done, so none of us can boast about it. For we are God's masterpiece. He has created us anew in Christ Jesus, so we can do the good things he planned for us long ago" (Ephesians 2:8-10 NLT).

My life before Christ was much like one of my nephew's puzzle attempts. I forced pieces into places they didn't belong, frustrated with how the picture was turning out, walking away and starting a new puzzle, bringing with me old pieces to a new puzzle, mixing old puzzle pieces with a new one. The picture was ugly and nothing like I imagined. But turning to Christ, choosing life in Him, He sorted out the pieces and helped me start with a new perspective.

Will You Choose Him?

A puzzle is not complete without the final piece. If you have been trying to shove other pieces in your life and they just don't fit, or if there is a missing piece, it's time to choose Jesus. You can pray this prayer even now.

Lord Jesus, for too long I've tried to put the puzzle pieces together myself. I know I'm a sinner and can't save myself. I cannot figure this life out myself. By faith, I gratefully receive Your gift of salvation. I am ready to trust You as my Lord and Savior. Thank You, Lord Jesus, for coming to Earth. I believe You are the Son of God who died on the cross for my sins, rose from the dead, and ascended into heaven. Thank You for bearing my sins and giving me the gift of eternal life. I believe Your words are true. I trust You

with my life. I invite You to lead and guide me, today and every day. Amen.

6

This Is All About a Life on Purpose

Daniel Rhea

"Many are the plans in a person's heart, but it is the Lord's purpose that prevails"

(Proverbs 19:21 NIV).

When I was younger, my family took a bike ride on the Katy Trail. Like most nine-year-old boys, I was pretty sure I was a professional BMX rider. I could keep up with anyone. The training wheels were just for show. Obviously. My dad was pulling my two sisters in a carrier with his bike, but I was a man, so I was riding just ahead of them.

Suddenly, I hit a bump in the road. My handlebars took a wild jerk to the left. It shot me like a slingshot—straight toward the edge of a bluff. I just knew I was headed for disaster.

Of course, the way I remember it, that cliff was at least 200 feet high. There were violent, crashing waves at the bottom of it and sharp, killer rocks beneath those. As an adult, I asked my dad about that bluff. He told me it was really a small one. Go figure. Still, at that moment, as a nine-year-old, I knew there was great danger in the direction I was headed.

I was about to fall off that high mountain into the shark-infested waters below (it didn't matter that we were in Missouri—in my mind, *sharks*). But just before I would've tumbled over the side, I suddenly felt a sharp, saving tug on my bike. My dad had practically flown to catch up. He swooped in and saved me. Grabbed me just in time. Talk about dad reflexes. Now that I'm a dad myself, I understand those reflexes a lot better. They've come in handy for me too.

God's Direction

There will constantly be bumps in the road in life. We decide whether we will let our own desires take control and jerk us in the wrong direction, or if we will allow God's purpose for us to determine our direction. If I consistently follow the path my flesh wants me to take, I am headed straight for destruction. Sharp rocks and sharks. Nothing good that lasts will come of it.

The God of the universe, the One who spoke everything into existence, has a purpose specifically planned and designed for you. People say we're meaningless specks of dust in the universe, with pointless, short lives to live, going about our insignificant business doing unimportant things. How sad. How devoid of hope. There is a God, *the* God, who created you and loves you and wants to do awesome works through you. And me. So let's let Him.

A Life on Purpose

"Then Jesus told his disciples, 'If anyone would come after me, let him deny himself and take up his cross and follow me. For whoever would save his life will lose it, but whoever loses his life for my sake will find it'" (Matthew 16:24-25 ESV).

Living a life on purpose looks extreme, and we continually fight our fleshly desires. Purpose puts our wants aside to better follow Jesus. "For wide is the gate and broad is the road that leads to destruction, and many enter through it. But small is the gate and narrow the road that leads to life, and only a few find it" (Matthew 7:13-14 NIV). It looks like choosing the narrow road—the road that's far less traveled.

The Narrow Road

On this narrow road of living life on purpose, what do you think we might find? In Matthew 16, before Jesus told His disciples to take up their cross, He told them He was going to be killed. Peter pulled Him aside at that and tried to talk Him out of it. "'This shall never happen to you!' Jesus turned and said to Peter, 'Get behind me, Satan! You are a stumbling block to me; you do not have in mind the concerns of God but merely human concerns'" (Matthew 16:22-23 NIV).

Jesus was on the narrowest of roads. He had to have been stressed to the max. And then here comes Peter, trying to keep Him from living out God's will for His life. Jesus called him His "stumbling block."

We all have places in our lives where we're more susceptible to tumbling over the edge and into sin—places that could jerk us onto a wrong path, situations that could cause us to stumble. Maybe even as you read this, a couple of your own places of susceptibility pop into your mind. It's our job, as Christ-followers seeking to live a life on purpose for our God of me, to deny ourselves. To put behind us the things that make us stumble and allow Him to do in us what we can't. If you struggle with alcohol, you can throw away the bottle. If you struggle with porn, you may even have to throw away the computer. If you struggle with following the wrong people, God might be calling you to stop putting yourself in their path—maybe even end some relationships.

Yet living a life on purpose is not losing. It's finding life and finally finding the joy of doing exactly what we were created to do. We weren't created to sin, to find momentary, pointless satisfaction. We were created for something far more satisfying, a life lived on purpose. Eternal purpose.

Father, thank You for giving meaning to my life. Without You, life truly would be empty and without real purpose. But You've given me hope and so many reasons to have joy—all because of how You love me. Help me to live a life that is worthy of the purpose that You've called me to. Help me to live out that purpose in every area of my life. Amen.

7

This is All About Your Will Be Done

Micah Bartig

"Then he said to them, 'My soul is very sorrowful, even to death; remain here, and watch with me.' And going a little farther he fell on his face and prayed, saying, 'My Father, if it be possible, let this cup pass from me; nevertheless, not as I will, but as you will'"

(Matthew 26:38-39 ESV).

As humans, we are so temporal minded. Can you think back to a time in your life when you made a decision in haste that caused you much pain—maybe even had lifelong effects? I believe all of us have had that experience to some degree or another. It's because we so often think we know best.

If you'd like to see the evidence, check out all the differing opinions on social media. There are countless people giving their ideas and so-called insights—and sharing them as if they have great authority. Sometimes they throw the names of a lot of experts in there to back up their "facts" that aren't really facts at all.

The problem is, nobody has all the answers to life's questions, experts or no experts. The only one who has it all figured out is God.

In the passage in Matthew above, Jesus has been walking with His disciples. He leaves them behind to be alone with His Father. The prayer of Jesus in that alone moment is absolutely astonishing. He uses simple words, but with such powerful weight behind them. It's mind boggling when you consider Jesus was—in actual fact— God with skin on.

Jesus the Son, Talking to God the Father

In verse 39, Jesus prays, "My Father, if it be possible, let this cup pass from me; nevertheless, not as I will, but as you will" (ESV). He's praying, anticipating His arrest and death. Just eight verses later, we read of Jesus being betrayed and we see that arrest happen.

Jesus was fully God and fully man at the same time. We can't comprehend it, but we know it's true. It's right there in the Bible. Jesus came to the Earth "to seek and to save the lost" (Luke 19:10 ESV). He did that saving work by becoming the perfect sacrifice and dying on the cross so you and I might have life and "have it to the full." (John 10:10 NIV)

In the focus passage, Jesus was about to take on the sins of every human being—past, present, and future. We can't grasp that price. Jesus would, for the first time, be separated from the Father because of our sin. He would be separated from the Father just as we were before Christ. Jesus alone understood the pain, the price. Along with the agony of that separation, His human body would feel every nail, every lash, every thorn that would torture Him for our sake. Death on a cross was hours of pain and torment. It was a slow, agonizing, and gruesome death.

Jesus knew what He was about to experience. It makes sense that He would say, "Let this cup pass from me," doesn't it?

But there is an amazing revelation in the next sentence of Jesus' prayer. "Nevertheless, not as I will, but as you will." What if Jesus had stopped His prayer at the point of asking to be free of His burden? You and I would be hopeless. We would be stuck in our debt, owing more than we could ever pay to the sovereign Creator of the world, and we would suffer the punishment. Eternal damnation.

But Jesus did not stop there. Rather, He asked that God's will would be done and not His own. Wow! Jesus followed through with the will of the Father, knowing what it would cost Him.

How About You?

I want to circle back now to my original question. How has your life been affected by wrong choices, by seeking your own will instead of God's? If Jesus Christ did not insist on His will, we shouldn't either.

I am all for praying big and believing big because God tells us to do so many times throughout the Scriptures. But that doesn't mean everything we ask for is what God has for us.

This Christian walk is not always easy. Some Christians through the ages have literally been called to die for their faith. But all of us must learn to die to self. We're told in the Bible to put away the desires of our flesh. We need to daily seek to get rid of everything in our life that is contrary to God's will. We are called to be all about "His will be done."

That changes our prayer life. By the power of Christ working in us, we can learn to pray as He did. As a church and as individuals. As we allow Him to lead, we pray less selfishly. Our prayers become less about our desires and much more about what our God wants for us. With that change in our prayers and in our mindset, we find an abundance of joy, peace, and freedom.

Be encouraged, Church. We serve a God who is all-knowing and all-powerful, and He can take care of you. Ask Him what His will is for you. Ask Him what He wants to do in and through you.

God, let Your will be done in my life. I trust You know best for me and that You work all things for my good. So in the good times and the bad, help me trust You more. Give me a confident knowing—trusting Your work in my life. For Your glory. Amen.

8
So I Choose to Worship

Jared Prindle

"I am in the midst of lions; I am forced to dwell
among ravenous beasts—
men whose teeth are spears and arrows, whose
tongues are sharp swords.
Be exalted, O God, above the heavens; let your
glory be over all the earth"

(Psalm 57:4-5 NIV).

They say knowing is half the battle. And I have to agree. I might go further and say that knowing is often most—or all—of the battle. It's often not the facts of a situation that cause us the most amount of stress. It's the confusion surrounding the situation.

In 2017, I got sick. And not just sick, but sick-to-my-stomach, coming-out-both-ends, I'm-gonna-die sick (#sorrynotsorry for the visuals). I can remember sitting on the floor in our bathroom with every ounce of energy drained out of me thinking, *This is it. This is how it ends.*

I yelled to my wife, "FAAAIIITH!!!" *pause to catch breath* "Get Annabelle!" (she was only a few months old) "Get out! SAAVE YOURSEEEELVES!!!" My wife and I laugh now about that day, but I was serious at the time. It. Was. *Horrible.* I genuinely thought I was dying.

But the worst part wasn't so much the physical ailment. It was the fear, confusion, and anxiety that accompanied it. I've always told people I could more easily handle my hand getting chopped off than pain on the inside of my body. I say this because I could look at my missing hand and be in immense pain with an intense feeling of loss, but I would know I'm not gonna die from losing it. But when I don't know what's going on inside of my body? Sheesh! Count me out. I just do not have the strength to mentally handle it.

Turns out my sickness ended up being a terrible bout of food poisoning. However, it triggered some very serious issues in my body and psyche. It completely wiped out my good gut bacteria.

After that, it seemed like almost anything I ate would trigger another round of indigestion and pain, usually at two in the morning. And every time I struggled with the pain, an enemy demon posse pounced on my thought life. I prayed, but no miracle healing happened. I doubted whether God heard my prayers. From there, I doubted if I even believed God was real. *Am I just kidding myself? Have I been deceived into believing a lie?*

I bet you never thought some stomach issues could cause such an existential crisis. But in me, it did. In those moments, it felt like my mind was not my own, but a battleground of competing thought-armies, with each side engaged in total war, dropping emotional bombs with competing facts, blowing apart the landscape of my soul. I felt lost. I felt alone. I felt hopeless. I was immobilized mentally, and the indigestion was wreaking havoc on my body.

How could this happen to me? I'm supposed to be a pastor helping others. I thought. Yet, each night at around two, I would wake up with gut pain and go to war mentally for hours. This went on for months. It was the closest I've been to hell.

Why do I tell you this? Because this is where I learned what it meant to worship God. After a long period of letting your mind become a battlefield between Christian apologetics teachings and secular arguments, you become so fatigued you want to quit thinking altogether. Though I never struggled with suicidal thoughts, I could see how people could get to a place where they just wanted out of the war. I thank God He gave me another option to stop the thought-war in my head.

At the Table

Psalm 23:5 became real. "You prepare a table before me in the presence of my enemies" (ESV). I started soaking every night in a warm bath with worship music playing. Any thought that entered my mind that was argumentative at all, I simply ignored. It didn't matter if it was a really good Christian apologetic thought or a worldly temptation to despair. I did not engage in that level of battle anymore. To quote Martin Luther, "You cannot keep birds from flying over your head, but you can keep them from building a nest in your hair."

I evicted the battle from my head by learning to truly worship. I chose to only worship God in those times. And believe me, it was sometimes a battle to choose to worship, but I knew it was the only way to get a short bit of peace. I knew I had to simply and calmly engage my mind and heart in worshipping the Creator.

Turns out, this was the key to victory. I finally understood how Jesus could sleep in the storm (Matthew 8) and why Israel's greatest warrior, King David, wrote so many worship songs. They weren't disengaging from the battle. They were going to a higher level.

Slowly, I got stronger, mentally and spiritually. It was like lifting weights. God didn't take away the battle, but as I chose to worship Him, He strengthened me through it. I finally got some sleep, ate more carefully, and the two o'clock mental wrestling matches happened less often. When they happened, I knew how to handle them. I would draw a warm bath and turn on chill worship music (Bethel's "Starlight" album was a favorite), and I would praise God in the storm.

What Are You Going Through?

Maybe you're in a dark place and struggling with more mental illness than I can comprehend. You read this story and thought, "What a little baby! He doesn't know what true depression and deep anxiety feels like!" And that's true. I am a little baby (just ask my wife), and I don't know the depths of what others go through. Or maybe you're dealing with a much more severe physical sickness than I experienced, and you're laughing at my little tummy ache. I agree, it was small compared to what many are facing.

I can't experience what you're going through. But I can tell you that, should I face something bigger in the future, I know exactly what I'm trying first. I'm choosing to worship Jesus in that storm because it worked in the last one. I'm going to run to the Author of life, not to argue with Him, but to worship Him, and to let the "peace of God, which surpasses all understanding," guard my "heart and mind in Christ Jesus" (Philippians 4:7 ESV).

So now the choice is yours ... what will you do?

God, You said to humble ourselves and You would, in time, exalt us. You were the one who said we should cast all our cares upon You, because You care for us. You were the one who said that those who are weary and heavy laden could come to You and You would give them rest. This isn't our

idea. It's Yours. So we come, weary and heavy laden, seeking rest, and we choose to humble ourselves and worship You today. Jesus, You are the victory and the peace that we seek. You are what our soul longs for, because we were designed to worship You. May Your will be done in our lives as it is in Your heavenly heart. And may the God of peace soon crush Satan underneath our worshipping and dancing feet. In Jesus' name, Amen.

9

You Are the God of My Mountains

Kurt Parker

"Then the Lord will go out and fight against those nations as when he fights on a day of battle. On that day his feet shall stand on the Mount of Olives that lies before Jerusalem on the east, and the Mount of Olives shall be split in two from east to west by a very wide valley, so that one half of the Mount shall move northward, and the other half southward"

(Zechariah 14: 3-4 ESV).

Mountains are a major theme throughout God's story. We see Abraham go to sacrifice his son Isaac on Mt.

Moriah. We see Moses meet God on the top of Mt. Sinai and receive the Ten Commandments. We see Elijah call fire down from heaven on Mt. Carmel. We see Christ pay the penalty for our sins on the top of that bloody hill we call Calvary. So what is significant about these mountains?

There is a saying when hiking up a mountain that you never really know how steep it is until you put your nose right up against it. From a distance, everything looks easy to climb. There was a time I was hiking up Camelback Mountain outside of Phoenix. As we pulled up to the mountain, I thought it looked like an easy hike. I was quickly humbled as I realized the pillars of rock around the mountain hid the steep path, at times every bit of 90 degrees.

The One Who Overcomes the Mountains

The mountains in our lives can often be the same. It's hard to understand the difficulty of the terrain we're about to traverse until we're on the path itself. We often struggle on our own, don't we? We try to go it alone. We feel we have the might and courage to scale any hill, but we don't. But there's good news, because God is walking with us.

One of my favorite verses is 1 Peter 5:6-7. "Humble yourselves, therefore, under the mighty hand of God so that at the proper time he may exalt you, casting all your anxieties on him, because he cares for you" (ESV). Jesus cares for you. He asks that you bring Him the wounds from your journey up the mountain, because His heart is for you. When we lose a loved one or get world-shattering news from a doctor, or when we're struggling to provide for our family or feel like we can't take another step, God is there. He gives us the strength we need to carry on, to overcome those mountains. The stories of God showing up and overcoming our mountains—those are the stories worth telling.

The One Who Moves the Mountains

Mountains seem immovable, impenetrable, even insurmountable. Yet Jesus says that with the faith of a mustard seed we can move them. A mustard seed is about one to two millimeters in diameter. This tiny, seemingly insignificant seed. How in the world can this tiny speck move a massive mountain?

Jesus is reminding us that the smallest part of Him is stronger than the biggest part of this world. When we put our faith and trust in the work of Christ, we can move any mountain. My favorite worship song is "Highlands (Song of Ascent)" by Hillsong United. The entire song speaks to my heart, but there is a line that seems to always speak louder than the others. It's about praising Him on the mountain, praising Him when the mountain is in the way, and praising Him because He is the summit. And our feet are right there.

I think about that and what it means to have the faith of a mustard seed. That whether I'm on the mountain or standing before it, that Jesus is the summit where I long to stand.

This mountain cannot overcome You, Jesus. In fact, You overcame all mountains when You conquered them on Golgotha some 2,000 years ago.

The One Who Splits the Mountains

Have you ever picked up a rock and tried to break it in half using only your hands? You may try with all your might to split that rock, but I'm here to tell you it's impossible. Yet in the future, the Creator will return to His creation, and when He returns, He will land on the Mount of Olives, and He will split that mountain in half. Not a rock the size of His hand, but an entire mountain. When I say split, I'm not talking about a tiny hairline fracture, but as we read in our opening passage in Zechariah, Jesus splits the mountain with such force that half of it moves north and the other half moves south, creating this massive valley that runs east to west. The thought of this leaves me breathless.

Our God is the One who splits the mountains. That should give you both a sense of fear and comfort, knowing this is who your God is. Regardless of any mountain standing in our way or any storms beating against us, we have a God on our side who will split those mountains and calm those storms, because He is Lord. He is sovereign. He has all authority, power, and dominion over the world, and He cares for us.

Why does God meet us on mountains? I think it's because it takes the journey up the mountain to know the power it takes to overcome it. When Elijah called fire from heaven, the journey he took to get there made that moment of God's power even more incredible. When God met Moses on Mt. Sinai, Moses had remembered God's faithfulness, and it brought hope and perspective to the rest of the journey ahead. Abraham wrestled as he walked his son up the mountain to be offered, yet his faith in the goodness of God and His promise pushed Abraham onward, until God's goodness was once again revealed. As we read that story, we know that nearly 1,900 years later, God would offer His own Son on a hill as a sacrifice for us all.

We climb the mountains in our lives so God can prove to us He has the power to overcome them, the power to move them, and the power to split them in half if need be. No matter how steep the terrain is ahead, no matter how tough the journey may look, God has you. He won't leave you to suffer the mountain alone if you will come to Him for help. He will walk step by step with you and give you the strength to overcome. Don't give up, don't lose hope, because the one who splits the mountains is the God of your mountains.

Jesus, thank You for walking with me up these mountains. Thank You for overcoming, moving, and splitting them. Thank You for proving over and over again that Your heart is for me. Thank You for the hope I have in the assurance of the cross, and thank You that the hope You give

will push me to face any mountain that lies ahead, because You are the God of my mountains.

10

You Are the God of My Seas

Autumn White

*"Moses answered the people, 'Do not be afraid.
Stand firm and you will see the deliverance the
Lord will bring you today ... The Lord will fight
for you; you need only to be still'"*

(Exodus 14:13-14 NIV)

In August of 2019, my husband and I had been coming to NorthRoad for almost four years. Within those four years, God completely changed our lives. When we first walked in those doors, I was barely 21, we weren't married, and we had a baby. The list of troubles goes on and on. But I had seen God's power transform me.

Still I was feeling a little lost—like I was wandering through the wilderness in my relationship with God. I was a mom of two girls, a four-year-old who was getting ready to start preschool and a six-month-old I had been home with since her birth. We were struggling a little financially, and I was wrestling with the need to go back to working full time. It would mean I would work mornings while my husband worked nights. I was wandering in new, uncomfortable territory.

What does the wilderness look like to you? What does it feel like?

My Wilderness

Looking back, I realize now much of my struggle was because I held onto the feeling I was unworthy. In those previous years, I had seen God fight some major battles for me. But at that point of struggle, I felt far from Him. I thought I had to accomplish all the items on some crazy checklist, maybe make my way through some huge obstacle course, and earn my way to knowing what He wanted me to do. I knew God had something He intended for me, but part of me thought I didn't deserve it. Like I didn't even deserve to know what it was. I didn't know if I could check enough boxes, do enough, or do it all well enough, to be worthy of what He had in store for me. It reminded me of the Israelites in Exodus.

The Israelites had seen God's power through the plagues, and when they finally found freedom from the Egyptians, God went ahead of them in a pillar of cloud and fire, guiding them and leading the way. In Exodus

14:10-11, we see the Israelites terrified and blaming God for bringing them to the desert to die.

I read this passage and thought, *How do you Israelites not see that God is with you? That He is surrounding you and making a way for you?*

But wasn't I doing the same thing? I was doubting who God says I am. I was losing faith because I felt unworthy. What God did next shows the nature of the true God of my seas.

The God of My Seas

"Raise your staff and stretch out your hand over the sea to divide the water so that the Israelites can go through the sea on dry ground" (Exodus 14:16 NIV). God is talking to Moses. He uses Moses to divide the waters for the Israelites so they can cross through the sea at just the right time. He did this to save them from the Egyptians. He did it to gain glory through Pharaoh.

God was with me all along in the same way, guiding me through the wilderness to an opportunity to work in ministry. I didn't feel worthy or qualified to do the ministry job, but my worth isn't in who I say I am. My worth is in who God says I am. When I was asked if I would be interested in working in ministry, my first answer was no. Everything inside of me was telling me I couldn't do it, that the church needed someone better for the job. But God. I love that I'm able to say that. And I love constantly hearing how God has changed lives.

I was broken, but God. I was lost, but God. I had no hope, but God.

Add your story there, and then add the "but God." As for me, God has given this amazing opportunity to work in ministry. He's given me a life that's so much better than the one I tried to plan myself.

I didn't feel qualified to do the work I do, but He is equipping me. It's not always easy, but He goes before me, and He is always with me. And through the journey, I've discovered that taking the leap of faith to do something I had never imagined possible is not the end of what God has planned for me. It is just the beginning.

How About You?

As you go through your day, think about what God has done for you and where your self-worth comes from. There will still be times of wandering through the wilderness—or maybe you're wandering right now. It's important how we respond in those moments. Are we seeking the things of this world and a quick fix for the unsureness of those moments? Or, are we trusting that God has something planned for us? The next step of simply trusting God might just be the beginning of what God wants to do in you and through you.

Do not be afraid. Stand firm. God will fight for you. Be still.

God, thank You for who You are. Thank You for being a God who wants me just as I am, and that even through my unworthiness, You call me worthy. I ask You to give me the courage and strength to follow You—especially when I'm in the wilderness. Help me see You moving and working in my life today. God, give me the wisdom to be still in You and to trust You with my life. May I desire Your will over mine and surrender to You rather than trying to control. Amen.

11

You Are the Resurrection Voice Claiming My Victory

Allie McMullin

"But thanks be to God, who gives us the victory through our Lord Jesus Christ"

(1 Corinthians 15:57 ESV).

A few months ago, I gave birth to one of the most beautiful baby girls—probably in all of history. And, yes, I may be a bit biased, but that doesn't make it untrue.

Being pregnant this time around, I got to see my two older girls' reaction to my quickly growing belly. Some of those experiences were so sweet and tender. Like when Emerson, my four-year-old, would snuggle my belly and talk sweetly to her baby sister. "Hi, baby. I love you. You can come out whenever you want." And, some of those experiences were ... not so pleasant. Like when Oswyn, my two-year-old, shoved her juice box's bendy straw into my belly button because "the baby was thirsty." Ouch.

I loved trying to navigate through my children's minds to see what they understood or misunderstood about pregnancy and birth. At one point, Oswyn let it slip that she thought the new baby was going to be able to "skate" after she came out. I'm not even really sure if she was thinking roller skates or skateboard. Either way, honestly, I was all for it. You could even say I was on-*board*. I know, I know, but just *roll* with it.

I also have to admit I may have used some of what they misunderstood to my advantage. I recall a time Emerson asked me why I got to have two ice cream sandwiches, and they only got one. My answer was simple mathematics: I was eating one for me and one for the baby. She didn't argue with that.

To be honest, at times, it was hard for me to wrap my head around the concept of birth, too. It really is pretty amazing! I often thought how crazy it was to have a unique, tiny life inside me. And then, given the right amount of time (plus all that unpleasant labor business), she would be born!

Born Again

It's understandable that children would have a hard time grasping the concept of birth. It can seem pretty complicated pretty quickly. Don't think so? Just try explaining it to a two-year-old.

I wonder if it was similar to the way Nicodemus felt after hearing Jesus talk about how only people who are "born again" can see the kingdom of God. He responded, I think, how most people would after hearing that for the first time: *Umm...what?*

Thankfully, Jesus broke it down and explained what that meant in the verse so many know by heart. "For God so loved the world that he gave his one and only Son, that whoever believes in him shall not perish but have eternal life" (John 3:16 NIV).

New birth. New life. Bigger. Better. Forever-er.

This new birth is not without cost. It has its own sort of labor pains. The gift Jesus offers meant Him giving *His* life on the cross. But death wasn't the end, it was a new beginning! The stone was rolled away, and the tomb was empty. No skates, simply a miraculous rolling.

Jesus claimed victory over death through His resurrection, giving hope to all who accept Him. "Blessed be the God and Father of our Lord Jesus Christ! According to his great mercy, he has caused us to be *born again* to a living hope through the *resurrection of Jesus Christ* from the dead, to an inheritance that is imperishable, undefiled, and unfading, kept in heaven for you, who by God's power are being guarded through faith for a salvation ready to be revealed in the last time" (1 Peter 1:3-5 ESV, emphasis added).

Nothing proved Jesus was God more clearly than the resurrection. Jesus is who He said He was, and He can do all He said He could do.

Life Change

After giving birth, my life, as well as the rest of my family's, changed. These sorts of things have long-term effects. Sometimes good, and sometimes not so good. I remember Emerson sitting down with me one day and saying, "Hey Mama, you know what's really funny? You don't have a baby in your belly anymore, but your belly is still *really* big!"

Thanks, kid. True, my deflated balloon-belly did not look the same. But the change that makes it all worth it is that I can now see my little baby girl's face—this precious new life God made. What a gift.

Jesus' resurrection changes things. His resurrection leads to our resurrection. Romans 6:4-5 says, "We were buried therefore with him by baptism into death, in order that, just as Christ was raised from the dead by the glory of the Father, we too might walk in newness of life. For if we have been united with him in a death like his, we shall certainly be united with him in a resurrection like his" (ESV).

Resurrection completed the redemption plan. And He shares that claim to victory with us, so we get to declare along with Paul, "When the perishable puts on the imperishable, and the mortal puts on immortality, then shall come to pass the saying that is written: 'Death is swallowed up in victory. O death, where is your victory? O death, where is your sting?' The sting of death is sin, and the power of sin is the law. But thanks be to God, who gives us the victory through our Lord Jesus Christ" (1 Corinthians 15:54-57 ESV).

We serve a risen Savior. Not a dead god, but an ever-living, all-mighty, death-defeating, sin-conquering God of all. God of me.

Sweet Jesus, I am forever grateful for Your death and resurrection. Thank You for being the resurrection voice that claims my victory. Help me walk in newness of life today and the rest of my days. I pray these things in Your name. Amen.

12

You Are My Hope When I'm Hopeless

Chantal Hite

"When we were utterly helpless, Christ came at just the right time and died for us sinners"

(Romans 5:6 NLT).

When I was 18, I was living in Springfield, Missouri while going to college. Just after I finished my first semester, one of my best friends from high school came to visit. We had planned a fun weekend full of adventures. First on the list—a trip to Table Rock Lake. It would take about an hour's drive in my old Buick Skylark, which had more miles than the average vehicle. That car had so many ticks and clunks you could hear me coming from several blocks away.

The day we set out was beautiful. The sun was shining. We were so full of excitement for what was to come. We left early in the morning, hoping to spend the entire day at the lake. But it soon became apparent that we had a problem. We were heading up a long, steep incline on the highway when it became sadly clear my little Buick was just not going to make it up that hill.

This was before either of us had a cell phone, and we were about halfway to the lake in the middle of nowhere. My little Buick slowed to a crawl. We found a place to pull off on the shoulder and coasted to the side where my poor car died and refused to start again. As two young girls barely out of high school, we knew nothing about cars. We checked everything we knew to check, put the hood of my car up, and then just sat there trying to decide what to do.

I hadn't thought to tell anyone where we were going that day. The last town we'd passed was quite a ways back down the highway, and to trump all of that, we didn't think to bring any money with us. We were hopelessly stuck. We needed someone to see our needs and to rescue us.

We sat there for about a half hour. We prayed God would help us. Naturally, it seemed the easiest solution would be for God to just make the car magically start working again. Every so often, we would try to start the car, thinking, *Maybe this time*. But every time we turned the ignition, the same thing happened. Nothing.

We were running low on hope that the car would magically start, so we prayed God would send someone to help us. We needed a rescuer. Maybe someone we knew would be out that way, a nice old lady would offer us a ride, or perhaps someone who knew something about cars would stop by and jiggle the right part and the engine would burst to life, freeing us from the pit we were in.

Hope Arrives

The longer we sat there, the more we realized we were hopeless. We had nowhere to turn. Finally, our long-awaited rescuer came. A middle-aged man pulled his truck in beside us and asked us if we needed some help. We didn't even think of any potential danger. God had sent this man. He looked over my car, found the broken piece, and told us there was an O'Reilly's back down the highway. We hopped in his truck and drove 15 minutes back to that parts store, not knowing how we would pay to replace the broken piece.

Once in the store, the clerk tested the suspect piece. Sure enough, it was broken. Beyond repair. Here we were with a stranger. Our car was miles down the road. Our home was even farther. We had no money. Nothing to give. No way home. We were hopeless. But God. God offers hope where there is none. He heard our prayers and answered. The clerk surprised us with the news that the part was actually from one of their stores. And it had a warranty. They would replace it for free. The stranger took us back to my car, replaced the piece, and we were happily back on the road.

The Real Repair

Our lives are like this. We're broken. Far from home. Stuck. We've tried it all. Begged God to come to our rescue and fix our broken pieces. Told Him how to do it. But God in all His goodness never leaves us broken and without hope. He never jiggles what's wrong so we can merely get by. He sent the greatest repair person, Jesus. At just the right time, Jesus came and offered His life to repair our brokenness. And He did it all for free. He offers us hope where there is none. We have no other way to pay the cost of our sins. Nothing to offer to cover the damage. All we have to do is get in and trust our lives to Him to take us exactly where we need to be.

Thank You, Lord, for giving me hope when I had nothing to offer. Thank You for giving Your life to pay the cost of my sins to make that hope possible. I ask You to forgive me for relying on myself and my own abilities or on others and their advice or wisdom. It's so easy to doubt Your

grace and goodness, thinking I know what's best. When all hope seems lost, help me believe You are all I need. I place my hope for today, tomorrow, and every day in Your hands.

13

You Are My Refuge When I'm Weak

Mary Brittan Burgess

"Therefore, in order to keep me from becoming conceited, I was given a thorn in my flesh, a messenger of Satan, to torment me. Three times I pleaded with the Lord to take it away from me. But he said to me, 'My grace is sufficient for you, for my power is made perfect in weakness.' Therefore I will boast all the more gladly about my weaknesses, so that Christ's power may rest on me. That is why, for Christ's sake, I delight in weaknesses, in insults, in hardships, in

persecutions, in difficulties. For when I am weak,
then I am strong."

(2 Corinthians 12:7b-10 NIV)

Growing up in Orlando, Florida, snow days were never part of my childhood. But a distinct part of my childhood was hurricane days. Instead of getting out of school for icy roads, we got out of school for winds of great strength and rain. This was just a normal part of Florida life for us.

Sure, there was always the unknown of "anything can happen," but that's why most Floridians have a spot in the house for stormy weather. A place away from windows and doors. In our home, I can distinctly remember it being directly under the staircase. It was a closet, most of the time full of random junk, but when a hurricane was approaching, it became our refuge. My parents taught my siblings and me to go directly to that closet when the bad storms blew in. It was the place where they knew we would all be safe.

As Christians, when we are going through the storms of life, people often say, "Don't worry, the Lord won't give you more than you can handle." But when we're tired, overwhelmed—done—those words are an insensitive platitude. Because in that moment, it feels like more than we can handle. It feels like the storm we're walking through will surely sweep us off of our feet while our life crashes before our eyes.

Why Would God Do This to Me?

But what if God allows us to feel this way? You might want to argue, "How could a sovereign God ever allow me to feel this way?" What if God allows us to feel this way so that we recognize our need for Him?

I think it's absolutely intentional that the Lord gives us more than we can handle. Something beautiful happens when we realize we cannot do it all on our own. As the storm passes and we come out the other side, the only person we could give glory to is God, because we know that there would have been no making it through that storm without Him.

In 2 Corinthians 12, Paul is talking about this exact subject matter. Paul was given a vision, and in verse seven, he states, "Therefore in order to keep me from becoming conceited, I was given a thorn in my flesh, a messenger of Satan to torment me" (NIV). Let's stop right there. Paul says he was "given" a thorn in his flesh. Paul is considering this trial as a gift from the Lord. What a mindset.

He says in verse eight, "Three times I pleaded with the Lord to take it away from me. But he said to me, 'My grace is sufficient for you, for my power is made perfect in weakness.' Therefore I will boast all the more gladly in my weakness, so that Christ's power may rest on me. That is why, for Christ's sake I delight in weakness, in insults, in hardships, in persecutions, in difficulties. For when I am weak, then I am strong" (NIV). Paul is rejoicing in his storm because he knows that when he humbles himself to admit he cannot do it all on his own, the Lord comes through for him.

Who is My Refuge?

Like hurricanes, when the storms of life come, what or who is your refuge? Is it that comfort food, that bottle, that drug, or staring into that bright screen that sits in our pockets every day? The problem with taking refuge in all of those things is that they leave us empty, unprotected, and anxious. It's like being in a room full of windows and doors in the middle of a storm. However, when we lean into the Lord as our refuge during the storm, we don't have to trust in our own abilities. This leaves room to let the Lord take over, resulting in us boasting in our weakness because we know the ONE who is our strength.

Taking refuge in Him now is like the little closet under the stairwell of my house, cozy and safe, allowing us to rejoice in the trials that have been placed before us. This is why if God is the "God of Me," taking refuge in Him is our only option. Otherwise, Satan is going to continue to use the lie that we can do it all on our own as a "little g god" of pride in our lives.

What part of your life do you need to let God step into and be your refuge today? Allow Him to be the "God of Me" right there.

Lord Jesus, help me today to take refuge in You in whatever storms are going on in my life. Allow me to rejoice in the trials and storms You have placed before me because I know You are my strength in these times. God, take away the idol of pride in my life in every place I've wrongly believed I can do it all on my own, so that I can fully trust You.

14

And You Restart My Heart of Hearts, You Are the God of Me

Greg McGhee

"Behold, I will open your graves and raise you from your graves, O my people. … And I will put my Spirit within you, and you shall live … Then you shall know that I am the Lord …"

(Ezekiel 37:12b, 14b ESV).

Early one morning in 1996, I was driving my 1989 Chevrolet S-10 back to college in Hannibal, Missouri.

I had gone home for the weekend and stayed late on Sunday night. I decided instead of driving home so late, I'd just stay there and get up early enough to drive back for my eight o'clock class. It was only an hour, maybe an hour and fifteen tops, to get back. I could handle that.

Bad decision. I made it about halfway. MODOT was widening Highway 61 into a four-lane, so they were building an overpass in Bowling Green. I was tired, kind of dozing even, when I looked up and found there were cars stopped right in the middle of the highway. Stopped!

I slammed on the breaks, but quickly realized there was no way I was going to stop in time. So I steered my truck over to the shoulder and continued to brake. The shoulder was short because of the construction. I knew I had to be quick.

I was so relieved when my truck finally stopped there on the shoulder—a good four or five cars in front of the last vehicle in the line. I turned my head sheepishly left and met the eyes of a worried-looking—and rather angry-looking—driver in the car parallel to mine.

Up to that point in my drive, I had struggled to stay awake. But from then on? Wide. Awake! With all that extra adrenaline, my heart jolted. The jump-start lasted all the way to Hannibal.

Restart My Heart

In Ephesians 2:1-2, Paul says, "And you were dead in the trespasses and sins in which you once walked, following the course of this world …" (ESV). Far worse than drowsiness or sleepiness, we were dead. When Jesus found us, we did not need an energy drink or a cup of coffee. We needed to have *life* breathed into our heart of hearts.

A story in Ezekiel illustrates this well. God takes Ezekiel to a valley full of dry bones. The words "dry bones" carry some pretty grotesque and vivid imagery. Not only were the people to whom these bones belonged dead, but they were long dead. Long enough for the flesh to rot off the body and the bones to dry out. These were not the bones of someone who'd been dead for a few minutes, could be given a jolt from a defibrillator, and then could come back to life. These were bones of people who had been dead for months, maybe years. The passage describes how the bones rattled, then tendons and muscles formed, then skin. And then God *breathed* life into the lifeless bodies.

This picture in Ezekiel and Paul's description in Ephesians tell the same story. Spiritually, we were dry bones. Without Christ, we had no hope of spiritual life. But God, in His mercy, reached out and raised us from spiritual death into spiritual life.

I love that after breathing life into the lifeless, God says, "Then you shall know that I am the Lord" (Ezekiel 37:14 ESV). It's so like our declaration, "You are the God of me!" *You, God, are my God. You are the Lord.*

Declaring that God is the God of me is not about saying God is Lord. He is Lord whether or not we announce it. Rather, as we declare He is the God of us, we are acknowledging and surrendering to the truth of who He is.

Philippians 2:10-11 says, "So that at the name of Jesus every knee should bow, in heaven and on earth and under the earth, and every tongue confess that Jesus Christ is Lord, to the glory of God the Father" (ESV). Jesus is Lord. That's a fact. He is your Lord. And that's true—whether you acknowledge it now or later.

Have you surrendered to that lordship? At the moment of surrender, God breathes life into your lifeless body. That's where you begin to really live. It's where you find abundant, fulfilling, and purposeful life!

God, thank You for sending Your Son to die on the cross so we can know what it means to have life. Without You, I am dead and hopeless. I am dry bones lying in an abandoned valley. I desperately need Your breath to fill me up and bring me back to life. I know it's only possible in You. I hear You asking me the question You asked Ezekiel. "Can these bones live?" Even now, I answer with confidence, "Yes!" Awaken my spirit to Your presence and breathe life into my breathless lungs, God. Amen.

15

You Are the Grace for the Journey

Rhonda Rhea

"Therefore let us [with privilege] approach the throne of grace [that is, the throne of God's gracious favor] with confidence and without fear, so that we may receive mercy [for our failures] and find [His amazing] grace to help in time of need [an appropriate blessing, coming just at the right moment]"

(Hebrews 4:16 AMP).

I stood there looking at the car, shaking my head in utter disbelief. Disbelief and no small amount of judgment. That driver needed to be at least a little bit shamed. *Pull the car in. Into the plainly marked spot. Put it between the two yellow lines. That's all you had to do. It's parking, not rocket science. How could anybody mess that up?*

I should mention at this point that it was me. I was the driver who had messy-parked that car. I messy-parked it big. I never even noticed until I got back from shopping. Not only was the car practically on a sidewalk, but I had parked right on top of one of the yellow lines. Those bright, bright yellow lines. I was parking my little SUV-ette, not a Winnebago. What should've been a walk in the park came closer to a park on the walk. I might actually do better with rocket science.

Ordinarily, I get every kind of bothered when my tires are even close to touching a line. I avoid those stripes like a parking lot plague, and I usually make sure there are no tire-on-line breeches. That day, I didn't check. Though I might add here that neither tire was touching a yellow stripe. But it was because one line was almost smack-dab center of my car. Like a field goal. How embarrassing.

There's only one thing a person can do at that point, right? Jump in the car and speed off before anyone sees that you're the one who parked it. I practically squealed those tires. My Equinox was suddenly the Batmobile. It's true that instead of fighting crime, I was trying to lessen my parking disgrace. That makes it even more ironic that I forgot about the speed bump on that lot and pretty near concussed myself.

Getting a Line on Grace

Isn't it glorious that our Jesus has grace for every disgrace? He has compassion for every place we completely miss the mark. He has compassion as well for every affliction we encounter in this sin-cursed world. His is not the compassion someone feels from afar. It's a grace that comes near. One that's personal. A grace that touches.

In Jesus' time walking this planet, He met a man with the humiliating plague of leprosy. The man came to Jesus and begged for healing. "Moved with compassion, Jesus reached out his hand and touched him. 'I am willing,' he told him. 'Be made clean.' Immediately the leprosy left him, and he was made clean" (Mark 1:41-42 CSB).

Oh, these words: "Jesus ... touched him." He touched him! Touched this unclean person. The man was breaking ceremonial law to even be there. He wasn't supposed to come near anyone at all, much less a crowd. But instead of doling out judgment and shame, our Savior was "moved with compassion." Moved to ignore the law that would keep the leper at a distance. Moved to ignore the law that forbade Jesus to touch him.

Touched Truly Touched by Grace

It's that same compassion that brought Jesus near to the whole world. We were all defiled, unclean, humiliated—we had all missed the mark. Our perfect Savior touched sin on our behalf, taking it upon Himself, becoming our defilement so we could be made clean—*soul clean*—and have a wondrous relationship with a holy God.

So that He could become, in the most personal touch, God of me.

He gives grace for our journey through this life—however crazy-parked we find ourselves. Our God is gracious beyond anything we can imagine. And it's not so much that He has decided He will show grace. But it's that grace is simply who He is. He IS our grace. Every time I contemplate the God of grace, it makes more and more sense for me to recognize, follow, serve Him as the God of me.

I'm going to park right here and think about that today. In His limitless compassion, He comes near. He touches. Grace for every disgrace. Grace that, I dare say, redraws the lines.

Father, thank You for Your grace. Thank You for not merely doling it out here and there as we might happen to do something positive, but for lavishing it on us where we don't deserve it. Lavishing it in all those places we've earned the exact opposite. Thank You for pouring it over our biggest mess-ups and missed marks. Only Your grace can get us through this life journey. I bow before You even now, recognizing that You—YOU are the God of me.

16
You Are the Promised Victory

Matt Bartig

"I have told you these things, so that in me you may have peace. In this world you will have trouble. But take heart! I have overcome the world"

(John 16:33 NIV).

In moments of struggle, what is your go-to for comfort in the storm? Do you like food? Netflix? Sexual distractions? Projects at home? Projects at work? We all have different sources of comfort—some are fine, some are not. They are our go-to comforts for helping us forget our present troubles.

Ahhh, forgetting the present. Maybe you were pretty thrilled to think about forgetting your troubles. That might sound really good right now. Maybe your stress level is maxed at a ten. Maybe you're feeling utterly helpless, like there's no way you can overcome the obstacles in your life right now.

It's those feelings that can drive us to grab for creature comforts. Again, what are yours? What do you typically go for?

Did you know that what you go for in those moments says a lot about your heart? It might even reveal who is the God of you—or the god of you, little g. It's not even that all those go-to things I mentioned are always bad. They lose their value, however, when we reach for them *first*. Because that's a sign they might be our own little-g-gods. What we reach for in times of struggle many times holds the number one place of priority in our lives.

Why? I think it's because we believe those comforts are what will help us through—like those are what will give us what we need to live another day. We think if we have that (fill in the blank) thing, we'll be able to make it, or at least fake it 'til we make it. We feel if we have that one comfort, that's what will help us get by until the next, better day. So we make it our go-to, and then, maybe over time, often make it our god.

Instant Peace?

We need to understand something important. Most of us don't set out to follow other gods. What we really want in those weak moments is usually just a little peace! In our search for instant relief, we find other substitute remedies for our troubles. We search for a small victory, and instead we step into a battle with the devil that's so much larger than we are.

In the Bible, we find a harsh truth. It's in our verse for the day (above). We learn that in this world, we will have trouble. I know what you're thinking: *Thanks, Captain Obvious. I already know that all too well.*

Hang with me for a moment, though.

God promises that none of us can escape trouble. It's in all our destinies. But look again at that passage. Isn't it interesting that before we read about how we will struggle in this world, Jesus said He was telling us these things so we could have peace? It's like He's saying He's going to tell us beforehand that we're going to struggle so that when it happens, we find peace.

So God is asking you about the little battle you're facing today. The one that feels so big? The one that's completely overwhelming? That battle is inside a war He has already fought and thoroughly won.

You Win!

Don't miss this. God is saying that no matter how your little battle comes out, it can't eternally hurt you. It doesn't change the fact that the war is over and the victory is sure. The outcome of that battle will not follow you forever. It can't even touch your forever. He's already sealed that.

That means you can take a deep breath and think, with an eternal mindset, about the fact that whatever you are going through, God promises you ultimate victory!

So the next time you hit a struggle (and sorry, but we all know there will be a next time), and you reflexively reach for some kind of substitute comfort first for stress relief, I challenge you to think first. Get an eternal perspective. Don't make a god of something powerless and temporary. And don't find a place of numbness. You don't have to find a distraction or forget the present. Those empty things you may try to run to first are powerless to help you through. But not only does God have all power, He has already won. Find your comfort in your victorious God. At every place, you believe and trust in His promises, you will find new peace.

Pray this with me.

God, give me an eternal perspective. Help me see my current problems for what they are. So small compared to You. Please, God, don't allow my struggles or my reactions to them define me. Don't let me allow them to send me chasing after other gods. I want to trust in You alone. Please give me the strength to do that. In Your name I pray. Amen.

17

You Are the Power of Salvation

Shawn Ohlms

"For I am not ashamed of the gospel, for it is the power of God for salvation to everyone who believes, to the Jew first and also to the Greek"

(Romans 1:16 ESV).

Whenyou think about the word "power," what comes to mind? Do you think of the power wielded by some gargantuan, chiseled-from-granite bodybuilder? Do you think of the power displayed by a natural disaster such as a tsunami, earthquake, or tornado? Or perhaps, like me, you grew up watching *Home Improvement*, and when you hear the word "power," your mind immediately takes you to Tim Taylor pleading for "more power!" as he soups up yet another soon-to-go-haywire home project.

When Paul wrote this letter to the Romans near the end of his third missionary journey, he was talking about something completely different. He was referencing an almost inconceivable, divine power—one of which the Roman believers needed to be reminded. This is an awe-inspiring power. Power that, when on display, makes you question everything you've ever thought about power. One that makes you stop in your tracks, jaw fully scraping the ground, and stand simply amazed.

Think about the first time you stood on a beach and watched the sun set. Or maybe the first time you drove in the Rocky Mountains and understood the majesty before you. Awe. Wonder. Reverence. That is the type of power Paul was referencing. It is imperative in our journey to fully allowing the Lord to be the God of us we understand not only what true power is but also who actually holds that power.

Where's the Power?

In June of 1994, *The Lion King* was released and would eventually become one of Disney's highest grossing films of all time. Unless you have been living under Pride Rock, you've seen *The Lion King* at some point and can recall most of the scenes. There is one scene in particular which perfectly illustrates the dichotomy of the power we *think* we have and the power God *has*.

Simba, as most children do, disobeys his father's orders, leaves the comfort of his home, and ventures beyond the land the light touches. He finds himself in the elephant graveyard and has a treacherous encounter with Shenzi, Banzai, and Ed—the dreadful hyenas. Simba, riding the coattails of his father, who is the king of Pride Rock, tries to stand his ground and offers a pitiful roar to scare off the hyenas. The hyenas simply laugh off Simba's futile attempts until he lets out a ferocious, ear-curdling roar, immediately sending them scrambling. Simba, full of confidence, puffs his chest at his unmatched prowess; only to turn around and realize it was his father doing the roaring.

I often think of the times in my life when I've felt really good about myself. I've reached some milestone or accomplished some seemingly remarkable feat, only to realize it was the Father doing all the work. It is in those moments I have been forced to swallow my pride, fall to my knees in humility, and recognize that, apart from Christ, I am absolutely powerless.

John 6:44 says, "No one can come to me unless the Father who sent me draws him. And I will raise him up on the last day" (ESV). Understanding what the word "draw" means in that passage is paramount to understanding the power God has. The Greek word translated "draw" is *helkuo*, which means "to drag." Think of a net full of fish being dragged onto a boat. The fish have no part in the power behind the drag. In fact, they sometimes move in direct opposition of the drawing. That sounds eerily familiar, eh? Let's not think so highly of ourselves as fish being dragged in a net that we boast of the power we have. Rather, let us recognize the one doing the dragging and stand in awe of the power He displays.

Come Out

Then Jesus, deeply moved again, came to the tomb. It was a cave, and a stone lay against it. Jesus said, "Take away the stone." Martha, the sister of the dead man, said to him, "Lord, by this time there will be an odor, for he has been dead four days." Jesus said to her, "Did I not tell you that if you believed you would see the glory of God?" So they took away the stone. And Jesus lifted up his eyes and said, "Father, I thank you that you have heard me. I knew that you always hear me, but I said this on account of the people standing around, that they may believe that you sent me." When he had said these things, he cried out with a loud voice, "Lazarus, come out." The man who had died came out, his hands and feet bound with linen strips, and his face wrapped with a cloth. Jesus said to them, "Unbind him, and let him go." (John 11:38-44 ESV)

An interesting thing happened when Lazarus was resurrected. Read John 11:38-44 again and highlight, underline, or circle the incredible power displayed by Lazarus. Still searching? There's a reason for that. All of the power displayed when Lazarus was brought back to life came from a singular source. *The* source. As you read that passage, notice the only thing Lazarus did was walk out of the tomb. It was the Father who called him out. It was the Father who granted the power for Lazarus to be raised again.

He's calling us. He's calling you to come out. To wake up and experience new life. To walk out of the self-made tomb and understand what Lazarus experienced. To no longer be bound. To be set free. To truly understand the power of His salvation. In order to fully experience that, we can no longer rely on the gods we've created in this world. It's time to allow Him to be the God of us. To be the God of you.

Father, we pray we would be unashamed of the Gospel. Please give us the boldness to, in every circumstance, rest in Your power, understanding we are nothing apart from You. God, in the moments we are weakest, may Your power be perfected. Allow us to walk forward knowing the same power that raised Jesus from the grave is at work within us. Lord, we are flawed, broken, and imperfect people who are desperate for You to call us to come out. May we hear that call and experience eternal resurrection. It is through You and by You we experience that power. Amen.

18

In You I've Been Set Free

Greg McGhee

"For freedom Christ has set us free; stand firm there-fore, and do not submit again to a yoke of slavery"

(Galatians 5:1 ESV).

One of my favorite movies of all time is *Shawshank Redemption* with Morgan Freeman. One of the most thought-provoking scenes is the one in which Morgan Freeman's character, Ellis Redding, is escorted to the gates of the prison for release, all dressed up in a nice suit. He sets eyes on a sky without fences for the first time in decades. Redding ends up in an apartment Brooks, the prison librarian, stayed in when he got out. Tragically, Brooks had taken his life when he couldn't adjust to freedom outside of prison.

The scene takes viewers through Ellis' similar struggle. He gets a job bagging groceries. As he works, he motions to his boss and asks if he can use the restroom. His boss says, "You don't have to ask me every time you need to use the restroom, just go." But Ellis had been required for most of his adult life to ask for permission. As he struggles, he narrates the scene. "There's a harsh reality to face. No way I'm gonna make it on the outside. All I do anymore is think of ways to break my parole, so maybe they'd send me back. Terrible thing to live in fear. Brooks knew it, knew it all too well. All I want is to be back where things make sense. Where I won't have to be afraid all the time. Only one thing stops me. A promise I made to Andy."

Learning How to Be Free

Maybe you've heard stories like this. Those who spend 40 years in prison like Ellis Redding and Brooks often struggle to exist outside. They struggle with freedom. They have been imprisoned for so long, they simply don't know what to do with freedom. It almost feels foreign and wrong to them.

Unfortunately, many believers walk around this world this way. They are free. They've had their sentence pardoned. In fact, Someone else stepped in and took their punishment, but they still walk around as though they are enslaved.

Paul says, "It is for freedom that Christ has set us free" (Galatians 5:1 NIV). I struggled for a long time to understand that passage. It seemed like a "well, duh" kind of statement to me. But I think Paul is intentionally overstating the obvious. It is for *freedom* that Christ has set you free. He didn't set you free for bondage, slavery to sin.

Specifically, Paul was talking about circumcision. Circumcision was a controversial topic of the time. Some of the old-timers, Jews who had become Christ followers, wanted the new Gentile (non-Jewish) believers to be circumcised before they could follow Christ. It was a traditional Jewish custom. But Paul is reminding these people of the obvious here. God did not set you free to put you under a set of antiquated rules and regulations. He set you free to be free.

How Does That Influence Our "Now"?

So, what do you go back to regularly in your life? What is the sin you fall back into? What is the rule you think you have to follow to be accepted by God? At the Harvester Campus, I've often quoted a phrase I once heard, "Ours is an acceptance-based performance, not a performance-based acceptance."

Let's make this crystal clear. We have not been freed *to* sin. We have been freed *from* sin.

We want to earn it. When life is not going well, we think God is angry. As in, maybe He's angry with me for stealing that Blow-Pop from my buddy Ben back in fifth grade. Maybe that's why I lost my job. Or why my kid is rebellious. Or why my car broke down.

But God is giving you His best. Always. Every time.

Let's meditate on Romans 8:28. "And we know that for those who love God all things work together for good, for those who are called according to his purpose" (ESV). And again, let's meditate on Matthew 7:11. "If you then, who are evil, know how to give good gifts to your children, how much more will your Father who is in heaven give good things to those who ask him!" (ESV).

We all need to understand, though, that this is not a promise that everything God ever gives you will be easy. It's not a promise that you won't go through difficult times. It's not a promise that you won't experience loss. It is a promise that God will always work all things, good and bad, together for your good and His glory.

God, thank You for loving me more than I deserve or could imagine. Thank You for being my Father. Thank You for desiring good for me. Thank You for calling me out of sin. Thank You for pulling me back when I fall into sin. Thank You for the days I receive Your blessings and for the days I receive Your discipline, because I know You work all things together for my good. Help me give You glory for it all. Amen.

19

You Are the Activation Code for Your Purposes in Me

Richie Rhea

"I am the vine; you are the branches. Whoever abides in me and I in him, he it is that bears much fruit, for apart from me you can do nothing"

(John 15:5 ESV).

"Now to him who is able to do far more abundantly than all that we ask or think, according to the power at work within us, to him be glory in the church and in Christ Jesus throughout all generations, forever and ever. Amen"

(Ephesians 3:20-21 ESV).

It's so frustrating to forget a password. Did you hear about the programmer in San Francisco who had a small hard drive, known as an IronKey, which contained a digital wallet that held 7,002 Bitcoin? It had grown in value. It used to be worth a little "bit." But now? $220 million!

The problem was Mr. Programmer lost the paper he wrote the password to his IronKey on. The IronKey gives a user 10 guesses before it "self-destructs" and erases its contents. All of it. Gone forever.

Last I heard, he'd made eight wrong guesses. He decided to store his IronKey in a secure facility until the day when cryptographers can hopefully come up with a way to crack the complex password code. He said keeping it far away, locked up, also helped him not think so much about it.

Which is more important? Knowing and fulfilling your purpose, or having millions of dollars? The truth is, you can have all the money in the world and still be miserable. But people who know the reason they're here, and who can accomplish their purpose, will be fulfilled. Happy, deep-down fulfillment. Fruitfully rich. Rich in every way that matters.

What is the Code?

The big question is, how? How do we unlock our purpose and find the power we need to fulfill that purpose? In 1 Thessalonians 5:24, Paul said, "He who calls you is faithful; he will surely do it" (ESV).

We all suffer from a type of blindness. It's an inborn inability to remember the code, and an inability, therefore, to activate the code. Passwords are easy to forget. I'm an expert at forgetting passwords. But it's so much worse when we forget the spiritual password. And it's more than just having forgotten the key to fulfilling our purpose. Without Him, we are dead to it.

The activation code is Jesus. Trusting Him with child-like faith, turning to Him, activates the power of Christ in our lives.

There is something in us that has the hardest time grabbing hold of this simple, eternal truth.

Finish these:

"Believe in your _ _ _ _."

"Pull yourself up by your own boot_ _ _ _ _ _."

"Follow your h _ _ _ _."

"I think I c _ _, I think I c_ _."

We're taught this philosophy, yes, but it's more than that. It's ingrained in our thinking. We've all heard that "God helps those who help themselves."

Our Creator/Redeemer taught something radically different. He said, "Apart from me you can do nothing" (John 15:5 ESV). And He said that if we abide in Him, we will bear much fruit.

Are we to work? Hard? Are we to huff and puff our way up the hill? Yes, we are. But not under our own power. Not for our own glory. Paul said, "I worked harder than any of them, though it was not I, but the grace of God that is with me" (1 Corinthians 15:10 ESV).

Remember Jesus

Remembering certain great truths are invaluable. The most important truth is Jesus.

There is a kind of amnesia that brings about spiritual poverty. It is forgetting to look to Jesus, who not only is the giver of our faith, but the completer too. That's why Hebrews 12:1-2 tells us to run this race of life looking to the founder and finisher of our faith. There is an amnesia that can happen, a forgetting of the password. We forget to look to Jesus.

Jesus is the code. Prayer to Jesus is the activator. Faith in Jesus is the password. As we pray, asking Jesus to not merely strengthen us, but to *be* our power and strength—so that He receives all the glory—brings us great joy. It is our purpose.

What hill do you need to climb? What weakness do you need to overcome? Who do you need to be empowered to love as Christ loves? What is bothering you? What sin is killing you?

Jesus, I know and believe You can do far more abundantly than all I ask or even imagine, according to Your power at work within me, so that when I make it to the top of the mountain, You and You alone get all credit. All the glory forever and ever belongs to You. Amen. I know I can't. I know You can. I trust You. When my faith is weak, cause me to trust You more.

20

You Are a Shield for the Righteous

Melinda McDonald

"After these things the word of the Lord came to Abram in a vision: 'Fear not, Abram, I am your shield; your reward shall be very great'"

(Genesis 15:1 ESV).

"He made Christ who knew no sin to [judicially] be sin on our behalf, so that in Him we would become the righteousness of God [that is, we

*would be made acceptable to Him and placed in
a right relationship with Him by His gracious
lovingkindness]"*

(2 Corinthians 5:21 AMP).

As we dwell on the Lord as a shield for the righteous, it's good to examine not only the shield, but also righteousness. These two words may not seem significant, but as we look closely, we see they are a picture of the complete coverage the Lord gives us as believers. We can rest in knowing that whatever season of life we're in, God has us covered.

The Shield

We don't see people carrying around a lot of shields these days. But in biblical times, shields were a part of everyday life. Encountering someone bearing a shield was about as common for them then as encountering a police officer or firefighter is for us now.

The shield was a soldier's defense. It was usually made from thick wood glued together and covered with several layers of animal hide. The Greek word for shield is "thureos." It's a word that was used to describe a big door. So we're not talking about the wimpy kinds of shields we might call to mind. This thing was practically a door—so massive it could cover the entire body of a soldier.

God uses such beautiful imagery in the Bible. Isn't it beautiful to think of faith as this huge, door-sized shield? We are covered entirely in every situation.

Take Up that Shield

Just as the Roman soldiers had, we also have an enemy. Paul tells us in Ephesians 6:16, "In addition to all of these, hold up the shield of faith to stop the fiery arrows of the devil" (NLT). We have a God-provided protection from the attack of our enemy. What a privilege it is to carry it. When we do, we're battle ready. Our shield will protect us from those fiery darts from that enemy who comes to steal, kill, and destroy (John 10:10).

We're instructed to hold up that shield. Raise it. To hold up our shield is to show our readiness. We're prepared when we're holding up our shield, holding onto faith, and understanding the power of God to keep us.

In Genesis 15:1, God tells Abram, "I am your shield" (ESV). Abram had a relationship with his holy God, and that close relationship resulted in a shield of protection for him.

Righteousness is described in many places as behavior in line with divine law. To be righteous is to be free from guilt. Isn't it beautiful that when we accept Christ, we become the righteousness of God?

Our Shield of Righteousness

We are safe, protected, defended. Doubly so. God is a shield for the righteous, and righteousness is our shield.

Second Corinthians 5:21 tells the story. "He made Christ who knew no sin to [judicially] be sin on our behalf, so that in Him we would become the righteousness of God [that is, we would be made acceptable to Him and placed in a right relationship with Him by His gracious lovingkindness]" (AMP).

We are made righteous not because our behavior has lined up perfectly with God's divine law. It's not because we're free from guilt. We've done the opposite and we're guilty. Yet because of Christ's death on the cross, instead of seeing our guilt, when God looks at us, He sees the righteousness of Jesus. It's nothing we could earn. It's all the work of Christ, who became sin "on our behalf, so that in Him we could become the righteousness of God" (vs. 21 AMP).

There is no shield as impenetrable as the shield of a believing faith. Not only impenetrable but also eternal. God's declaration of righteousness over you is forever.

Paul said, "But now the righteousness of God apart from the law is revealed, being witnessed by the Law and the Prophets, even the righteousness of God, through faith in Jesus Christ, to all and on all who believe. For there is no difference; for all have sinned and fall short of the glory of God, being justified freely by His grace through the redemption that is in Christ Jesus" (Romans 3:21-24 NKJV). It's crystal clear that it's through faith in Jesus Christ that we have the righteousness of God.

I challenge you to live in the peace of knowing that in Christ, God has declared righteousness over you. Understand He is your shield of righteousness, both now and forever. You will be blameless and pure on Judgment Day, and until that day, God will not leave you defenseless. He provides the shield of faith that we can take up daily.

Father God, thank You for my shield of righteousness through Jesus Christ. Thank You for loving me enough to send Jesus to conquer sin and win the eternal battle for me. Thank You that through Jesus we are more than conquerors, and that nothing will separate us from the love of God in Christ Jesus (Romans 8:37-39). As we live each day, eagerly anticipating the day we see You face to face, help us use the shield of faith You have given us and be ever grateful for that underserved righteousness You have bestowed upon us.

21

You Are My Year of Jubilee

Daniel Rhea

"Consecrate the fiftieth year and proclaim liberty throughout the land to all its inhabitants. It shall be a jubilee for you"

(Leviticus 25:10 NIV).

While in college, I commuted several hours a week. So much driving. I decided to upgrade from my '00 Ford Taurus. That thing had already had run-ins with way too many deer. I shopped around and found an '07 PT Cruiser. It held all my music gear, ran well, and got decent gas mileage. Since my girlfriend, Olivia—now my wife—stayed with me through that phase, that means it was a chick magnet, right? Okay, maybe not, but I was happy with it.

I didn't have enough money for the car, so I borrowed some from my dad. I was working while attending school, and I tried hard to save as much money as possible. That meant living with my parents while I commuted an hour to school, sometimes six days a week.

Eventually, I paid that debt completely. That was the first time I had a debt paid off, and it was incredibly freeing. What a feeling. It meant I could start saving even more money for the future—and maybe even get a burger from McDonalds every once in a while. The possibilities were endless.

The Year of Jubilee

There's an occurrence in the Old Testament, the year of Jubilee. When I hear the word "Jubilee," my mind immediately goes to the old X-Men character. But I think I can say with confidence that's not what we're talking about here. So, what is it?

Count off seven sabbath years—seven times seven years—so that the seven sabbath years amount to forty-nine years. Then have the trumpet sounded everywhere on the tenth day of the seventh month; on the Day of Atonement sound the trumpet throughout your land. Consecrate the fiftieth year and proclaim liberty throughout the land to all its inhabitants. It shall be a jubilee for you; each of you is to return to your family property and to your own clan. The fiftieth year shall be a jubilee for you; do not sow and do not reap what grows of itself or harvest the untended vines. For it is a jubilee and is to be holy for you; eat only what is taken directly from the fields. In this Year of Jubilee everyone is to return to their own property. (Leviticus 25:8-13 NIV)

The number seven is of significance to God. On the seventh day we are to take a sabbath and rest. The Israelites would take a sabbath every seven years and not sow or reap their fields. Taking that sabbath rest seven times brought them to the 49th year. Then on the 50th year, they would reach a super sabbath. The year of Jubilee.

During the year of Jubilee, all debts were wiped away, slaves were freed, and people were to return to their homes and rest with their loved ones. They were putting all trust and rest in God.

What a great foreshadowing of what Jesus did for us.

When Jesus died on the cross for our sins, He wiped our slate clean. He paid off every debt we ever accumulated—even those from years and years of sinful living.

When I paid off even my small debt to my dad, I felt relieved. How much more freeing it is now to know we have a Savior who took our eternal debt, and completely wiped it away. No interest charged, no extra fees. Just a filthy soul washed clean by the blood of the Lamb.

Rest in Him

A large part of the year of Jubilee is resting. But it's not the kind of resting that leads to sitting on the couch with a bag of Doritos while you binge-watch *The Office*. No, I'm talking about a rest that's so much more satisfying. Rejuvenating, even. I'm talking about resting in the Lord.

How often do we put away the stress of work, family, relationships, and all the things going on in the world and find real, meaningful, spiritual rest in the Lord? Corrie Ten Boom said it well. "If you look at the world, you'll be distressed. If you look within, you'll be depressed. But if you look at Christ, you'll be at rest."

No one can provide rest like Christ. The hope He gives us for our future, His forgiveness of our darkest sins, the undeserved mercy He shows—that simply can't be matched by anything temporary this world can provide. But it's up to us to find intentional—maybe even scheduled—time to focus on Jesus. To pray, read His Word, and rest in His goodness. Because of Jesus, every day is Jubilee.

So, let's put the phone down, step away from the computer, put work in the background, and appreciate, thank, and truly "Jubilee" rest in Jesus today.

Jesus, thank You so much that we can find rest in You. You've paid off our many, overwhelming debts, simply because You love us. You've given us a way to be with You forever. Help us become more intentional about resting in You. We can never repay You for what You've done for us, but we can dedicate our lives to living for You, loving You, finding rest in You, and helping others do the same. We love You, Jesus. Amen.

22
You Are Always By My Side

Micah Bartig

"The Lord is my shepherd; I shall not want. He makes me lie down in green pastures. He leads me beside still waters. He restores my soul. He leads me in paths of righteousness for his name's sake. Even though I walk through the valley of the shadow of death, I will fear no evil, for you are with me; your rod and your staff, they comfort me. You prepare a table before me in the presence of my enemies; you anoint my head with oil; my cup overflows. Surely goodness and mercy shall follow me all the days of my life, and I shall dwell in the house of the Lord forever"

(Psalm 23:1-6 ESV).

Psalm 23 is easily one of my favorite passages in all of Scripture. It's such a beautiful picture of God's interaction with His children. Even though the words are often used at funerals, this is also very much a psalm for the living.

The 23rd Psalm is wonderfully ordered. Its three sections point directly to the Gospel of Jesus Christ. Verses one and two point to justification, verses three through five show us sanctification, and verse six brings us beautifully to eternal glory. I love that these are the exact steps a believer in Jesus takes to be reconciled back to God. Again, it's the amazing Gospel. And each of these sections reveal to us a close and personal God.

Justification

Justification is the word used to describe what happens to a person when Jesus cleanses that person of sin and is justified in the eyes of the Father. The justification picture is present from the very first words, when King David says, "The Lord is my shepherd; I shall not want." The Apostle Paul tells us in Romans 10:9 that if we confess with our mouths that Jesus is Lord and believe in our hearts that God raised Him from the dead, we will be saved. When David calls the Lord his Shepherd, he is confessing that the Lord is his Master.

Justification through Jesus requires that we too lay everything down and profess Jesus as our Lord. Everything. Paul said that he considered everything a loss compared to knowing Christ. Jesus wants us to give Him everything because He has something so much better for us. It starts with purification from all sin and a right and tight relationship with Him.

Sanctification

Sanctification is the word we use to describe the process of becoming more like Christ as we go through life. We're made clean by Christ when we're justified, and we receive the Holy Spirit. Then the Holy Spirit leads us to live well, convicting our hearts when we stray. Verse three of Psalm 23 says that he leads us in the paths of righteousness for His name's sake. That's an awesome picture of the Holy Spirit's leading us through life, teaching us how to honor God in all we do.

David moves on in this section with the heavy words, "Even though I walk through the valley of the shadow of death, I will fear no evil, for you are with me; your rod and your staff, they comfort me" (verse 4). Paul tells us in Philippians 3:10 that part of becoming like Christ is joining with Him in His sufferings. The Bible promises we will experience trials, sadness, suffering, and pain. But Psalm 23:4 goes to the very heart of this entire devotional. The simple words, "you are with me." What a comfort. You are always by my side.

David follows with the mention of walking through the valley of death with, "I will fear no evil, for you are with me."

I want you to know, Jesus is always with you. Wherever you are, whatever you've done, even whatever you will do, Jesus will still be there. As you walk through sorrows and trials, Jesus is there. If you lose a loved one, Jesus is there. If you make mistakes, Jesus is there. Until the end of time, and beyond, Jesus is there.

So in times of difficulty or weakness, there's strength and comfort as we remember we are being conformed to the image of the Son, and God's power is made perfect in our weakness (2 Corinthians 12:9).

Eternal Glory

From the moment after the fall, when Adam and Eve sinned in Genesis 3, God has been working His plan to reconcile humankind back to Himself. The result is the perfect ending: eternity with Him in heaven. David paints an impressive picture of this when he says that he will dwell in the house of the Lord forever.

Everyone will spend eternity somewhere. God has made a way for us to spend ours with Him. He sent Jesus to justify all who will call on Him. Because of His payment for our sin on the cross, we become like Him in His death, and then we are raised in glory with the Father forever and ever. What a cool passage this is!

So let's make it personal. Have you started this process? Has there ever been a time when you professed Jesus as Lord? If so, do you see yourself becoming more like Him every day? Have you gotten off-track, living to gratify yourself and your own flesh, or are you staying on the path, living to please Him? How blessed we are to serve a God who is King of the universe but personal enough to walk close by our side. And He will lead us!

Thank You, God, for always being by my side. Your Word says that You will never leave me or forsake me, and I pray You would give me the faith to believe exactly what You say. Help me know You are by my side and help me walk with You in trust as You lead me through life. Amen.

23

You Will Never, Ever Leave

Jared Prindle

"Then Jesus came to them and said, 'All authority in heaven and on earth has been given to me. Therefore go and make disciples of all nations, baptizing them in the name of the Father and of the Son and of the Holy Spirit, and teaching them to obey everything I have commanded you. And surely I am with you always, to the very end of the age'"

(Matthew 28:18-20 NIV).

I try to stay as biblical as I can in my life decisions. That might sound cliché since I'm a pastor, but it's not. As a Christian, the Bible is the written authority for my life.

I'm supposed to align my beliefs, thoughts, and words with what the Bible says.

This is easier said than done, because sometimes when what I want to say is not what God has said. You might think that happens less often for pastors. We're supposed to study the Bible consistently. But it happens to us—maybe even more often.

When you're a pastor and preaching in front of a large group of people, you want each of them to feel loved. You want them to realize how good God is. You want them to follow Jesus. So there's a temptation to say something the Scriptures don't actually say.

We often hear leaders from the stage or in Bible studies say, "God will always be with you. He will never, ever leave you." That's fine most of the time. But if we're not careful, we can throw that thought around to mean something Jesus never intended. The Scriptures don't actually say God will be with everyone forever.

What? It's right there in the verse above!

It's true. It *is* right there in the Bible verse above. And it *is* a part of a song I helped write—the song this book is all about.

Confused? Stay with me.

Context Is Key

If we're going to be a biblical people, we have to read the above verse in context. This means we must take into account all that's going on around the verse.

In this passage, Jesus is speaking to people who are worshipping and following Him. People who will take the message of Jesus to the world. Who are those people? His Church!

The only group of people on planet Earth Jesus promised to "never, ever leave" is His people—those defined by worshipping and obeying Jesus and who take the message of Jesus and His Kingdom to the world.

His promise means if you follow Jesus, you have heaven's favor upon you. You have the Spirit of God residing inside of you (1 Corinthians 6:19). You are a new creation (2 Corinthians 5:17). You are a child of God (John 1:12-13). And Jesus will never, ever leave you (Matthew 28:20).

Isn't that amazing? If you are in Christ, you are incredibly loved and favored!

It's crazy to think of the implications of this. Jesus did *not* promise His presence and favor upon the rest of the world. Jesus did *not* say He would be with everyone always. Jesus did *not* say He would be with the giants in your life. Jesus did *not* say He would be with the demons attacking your family. He did *not* say He would be with evildoers who don't know God (Matthew 7:23). He said he would be with His church, His beloved, His bride, as they walk out their mission.

But what if I don't have it together?

It doesn't matter! Read the verse that comes right before our focus passage for this chapter. Some of them doubted! Crazy, right? But Jesus didn't say, "I'll be with those of you who didn't doubt." He didn't exclude those who were struggling with the weight of it all, but said, "I will be with you always."

What's the Bottom Line?

If you're reading this devotional and you have never made Jesus the God of your life, I urge you to do so. It's life changing. It's eternity changing. When you accept Christ, you get a new identity (1 John 3:2). Your sins are washed away (Romans 6:6). You are given freedom (John 8:36). You are given hope (1 John 5:13-14). You are given peace (John 14:27). Because of what Jesus did at the cross, access to God and His kingdom is given to you (Hebrews 4:16). Will there still be tough times? Sure (John 16:33). But Jesus makes the promise to His church to never, ever leave them.

If you have already made Jesus the God of your life, then take heart. The promise of Christ's presence is for you! And God is not a liar. If He has spoken it, He will do it (Numbers 23:19). Even if you doubt. Even if you struggle. Even if you can't understand what He's doing in your current situation. Even if it doesn't look like you thought it would look. Even if you are scared. Even in betrayal. Even in heartache. Even when the money isn't there. Even if the world comes against you. If you are in Christ, you are a part of advancing the Kingdom of Christ. If you are in Christ (2 Corinthians 5:17), then He is in you (Romans 8:9), and He is with you (Matthew 28:20). Take heart, highly favored one, for the Lord of Hosts is at your right hand and you will not be shaken (Psalm 16:8)!

God, I am humbled because You have promised to stick with me through thick and thin. That You have tethered Your soul to mine is absolutely mind-blowing. You truly are the best friend I could ever ask for. Help me be a better friend to You, and help me to walk with You more closely. Help me share this friendship with others. Help me as I make disciples of all nations, baptizing them in the name of the Father, Son, and Holy Spirit, and teach them to obey You. Help our church to live in light of the reality that You will never leave us or forsake us. We love You. In Jesus name, Amen.

24

You Are the Judge of the Whole World, But You Are Father to Me

Kurt Parker

"For the Lord is our judge; the Lord is our law-giver; the Lord is our king; he will save us"

(Isaiah 33:22 ESV).

I feel like God gets a bad rap in our culture. He is often viewed as this vengeful being who sits on a throne and judges the world. The crazy thing is, it's true. He absolutely is those things, but what the world fails to understand is that those things about Him are good.

I was recently going through pictures of our family, specifically my kids. Wow, my heart was overwhelmed with love for those little people in my tribe. There is nothing on this earth I wouldn't do for them. Nothing I wouldn't do to make sure they're safe, taken care of—to see their faces light up with smiles full of crooked teeth. There isn't any part of me I wouldn't give to them.

Likewise, and in an even more perfect and extreme way, God feels like that about me. "What is man that God is mindful of Him," speaks the psalmist (Psalm 8:4 NKJV). Did you catch that? This all-powerful, all-knowing God is mindful of me. He cares for me? Well yes, He does.

When I became a dad nine years ago, God gave me an incredible view into His heart. There is nothing I wouldn't give up to care for and defend my kids. God is no different. God is the judge of the world, and that means He is a good Father to me. Let's think about how.

A Father Who Defends

We need to understand sin is real. Evil is real. The enemy is real. First Peter 5:8 says, "Be sober-minded; be watchful. Your adversary the devil prowls around like a roaring lion, seeking someone to devour" (ESV). The enemy steals, kills, and destroys (John 10:10). He hates you, he wants to kill you, destroy you, to steal you away from God. God is good, and because He is good, He stands in total opposition of that. He gives us His law, a way to live, not as some heartless dictator, but as our loving Creator who knows the best way for His creation to live. God has standards because He is good.

When God judges the world, He does so to destroy sin, the enemy, and evil once and for all. If He didn't judge evil, He wouldn't be good. It's true that as we read passages about God's judgment, those passages should sober us to the reality of the kingdom of darkness. But they should also give us the hope that God will destroy those things that grip the world in darkness, and by doing so, He will set us free. Wouldn't a good father do that for his children? I know if evil was prowling around looking to devour my children, I would stop at nothing to destroy it. I would eliminate the threat. God's holy and righteous judgment of the world is good news for His children.

A Father Who Sacrifices

The hope found in God's judgment of sin is the cross and resurrection of Jesus. God's heart is for us. He desires to be in relationship with us as it was in the Garden. He desires it so much that He gave up His son so we could have union with Him once again.

I think of C. S. Lewis' incredible work, *The Lion, The Witch, and the Wardrobe.* In the story, the White Witch deceives and tricks one boy, Edmund, into betraying Aslan, the great King of Narnia. Because of the law of the land, Edmund would have to die for his crime of treason against the King. However, Aslan loved Edmund. So Aslan took Edmund's death sentence upon himself to save the young boy. Edmund deserved to die. He did nothing to earn what the King did for him. Aslan was willing to die because He loved Edmund.

My favorite verse is Romans 5:8. "But God showed His love for us in that while we were still sinners, Christ died for us" (ESV). Your Father loves you. He has shown His great love for you by giving up His life even while you were less than.

My kids do some boneheaded stuff. They take after me there. But nothing they could do would ever stop me from loving them. Nothing would ever stop me from giving up my life for them. Nothing stopped your Father from doing the same for you.

Father to Me

Being Judge of the world means God is a good Father to me. If He weren't the perfect judge and didn't have a standard for good and evil, would He be good? If He didn't judge the world, the sacrifice of Jesus wouldn't have meant anything. That God judges the world means His ransom for my life was the greatest act of love in history.

God must judge the world because through that judgment He will restore all of creation. He will reverse everything back to the way He intended it to be in the Garden. We will be His people, and He will be our God. He is our perfect Father. He is Judge to the world, but He is Father to me.

Father, I'm sorry for my rebellion. I'm sorry for not trusting You. God, thank You for providing us with all we need. Thank You for defending us from evil. Thank You for giving up Your life for me when I was still wayward. God, forgive me and restore our union. I know that life with You is better than anything this world could offer. I love You. Thank You for loving me. You are a good Father.

25

So I Stand Amazed in the Presence of Jesus the Nazarene

Autumn White

"My mouth will tell of your righteous acts,
of your deeds of salvation all the day;
for their number is past my knowledge.
With the mighty deeds of the Lord God I will come;
I will remind them of your righteousness, yours alone"

(Psalm 71:15-16 ESV).

Have you ever told your story? Your description of what God has done in your life? You might think you don't have a testimony. You might just be starting your relationship with God as you're reading this devotion. You could ask yourself, "Who would I tell my story to?" You might think your story isn't really interesting. You might be ashamed of your story and never want to talk about your past again.

I want to tell you a little bit about the first time I shared a part of my testimony.

Our wedding day.

August 6, 2016

"Nathan and I are already married. We got married on June ninth. Let me tell you why we choose not to tell anyone until today. Nathan and I attended church at NorthRoad since we first moved to the area, and within a couple months, God started to convict us of sin in our relationship and about not being married. So today this wedding isn't for me or for Nathan or for anyone else—except God. We want God to form the foundation of our marriage. We want God to be the rock where we build our relationship. We know that if God is the center of our marriage, our relationship will be one built on love, patience, kindness—and we know God will give us the strength to always choose to love each other."

This was the story I told on our wedding day. It was my first time telling anyone what God had done in me.

That day was one of the scariest of my life. I was nervous about standing in front of all our family and friends and telling them what we did and why we chose to do it that way. But what I remember more about this day was that in the middle of the chaos going on in my mind and heart, God spoke to my heart, "Stop. Remember who this day is about."

When I think about the feeling I had in God's reminder, I'm overwhelmed by His power and love. God stopped me in the middle of everything to remind me that our wedding wasn't about anything or anyone else other than Him. That thought gave me such peace about it all, because I knew, with God in control, I could do anything. I knew His victory would always be bigger than anything I could make happen if I was trying to control the outcome.

Testify

When I encourage you to share your story, I don't mean you have to do what I did or the way I did it. If you want to share it with a crowd of people, that would be awesome. But if the idea of standing in front of a hundred people to tell them how God has changed your life terrifies you, I get it. For Nathan and me, it was something God was calling us to do. His timing was clear and vital in this opportunity for His glory to be shared among several people who would probably never step foot in a church. That was something I didn't even realize He was doing until years after. It wasn't like I had planned for that to happen. If I remember correctly, the day before the wedding, Matt Bartig was the one who encouraged us to share at our wedding.

Your testimony is powerful—even if you don't know it. Have you ever thought about what God thinks when you share your testimony? I can only imagine the joy it must bring Him. It makes me think of my daughter. When my daughter tells other people about something I've done for her that made her feel loved or special, it's an overwhelming, lovely feeling. I feel proud of her for recognizing someone other than herself. I feel more loved by her because she is honoring me with her words. That must be a mere fraction of what God probably feels when He hears us sharing with others about what He has done in our lives.

But will my testimony make a difference for anyone?

What will people think of me when they hear about my past?

I'm so ashamed of what I did back then—why can't I have a different story?

Paul puts our questions and worries in perspective in 2 Timothy 1:8. "So do not be ashamed of the testimony about our Lord or of me his prisoner. Rather, join with me in suffering for the gospel, by the power of God" (NIV).

I had those questions and those very thoughts so often, too. But since I started sharing my story with others,

I have seen God bring people to me who needed to hear my story. People who were struggling with something they didn't feel they could share with anyone. But because of my vulnerability—because of my story—those people could open up about what they were going through.

For the longest time, I didn't want people to know my struggles because I didn't want them to think badly of me. But they haven't. They haven't thought me a terrible person for the choices I made in the past. They now see the power of my God showing up in me—and they see how He truly can change anyone.

Your testimony isn't for you. It's for others—so they can experience that same love and grace you have received from your Father. It is for God to bring people to Him. How amazing!

God, thank You for being a God who redeems. Thank You for Your grace in my life. Give me the strength to share Your power and love with others. God, if Your will allows, bring someone to me who needs to hear my testimony; and give me the wisdom to let You speak through me in those moments. Amen.

26
The Author of Creation

Allie McMullin

"Lord, you are great. You are really worthy of praise. No one can completely understand how great you are"

(Psalm 145:3 NIrV).

I am the daughter of an author. My mother has been writing for as long as I can remember. She's written over a dozen books and has been published in countless newspapers and magazines. I grew up watching her typing away on her computer to meet her deadlines. I listened to her at her speaking engagements, where she put a voice to many of the chapters and articles she had written. You'd think I would know a thing or two about being an author.

I remember a time in my elementary years when I thought I knew all about being an author. So much so that I took on the task of writing an article. After all, I'd seen my mom do it hundreds of times. I knew her formula well. Start off with something funny—maybe a silly story or some sort of illustration. Then move on to the lesson part where you find the takeaway message— insert appropriate Bible verse here. And finally, tie it all together by maybe referencing the joke in the beginning … annnnnd, done. Easy peasy.

So there I sat, seven years old, summoning all the wisdom I had garnered from those seven years of life experience to take on writing my first article. My chest swelled with pride as I sat down at the computer. I just *knew* it was going to be amazing.

I worked diligently. Typing 10, maybe even 11, words per minute with my two index fingers, eyes straining at the computer screen as I tried to recall all my second grade English lessons, making sure there were no grammatical errors. I had the most brilliant idea. I was positive this article was going to be funny and interesting, deep and profound, gripping and thoughtful. In my mind, the whole world was just waiting for *my* article.

What a Disappointment

When I finished, I ran over to the printer and waited to pick up my masterpiece. As I pulled the paper off the machine, I stopped and stared at the words I had written. Confusion took over my head space. *Wait, this can't be the article I worked so hard on.*

I had labored so long over that thing. I studied the words on the paper. Nope, that *was* my article. But the entire thing didn't even fill up half a page. And it was double spaced.

I read through my pathetic-looking article. Oh man. The part that was supposed to be funny and draw the reader in? Not actually funny. And the deep, life-changing lesson? Well, not all that deep, and definitely not life changing. When I was writing it, it seemed so brilliant. How was this possible?

My whole plan in writing the article was to teach the world a beautiful lesson, and then, of course, allow everyone to marvel at my wonderful creation. Instead, I took my disappointing piece of paper and hid it in my parents' basement. I hid it! It was a bit frustrating that I couldn't just throw it away, but I had worked waaaay too hard on it for that. No way was I going to let anyone read it.

What a Beginning

Have you ever worked so hard to make something you were sure was amazing, but found out later ... not so amazing? When God creates, it's nothing like that.

Nehemiah 9:6 says, "You are the Lord, you alone. You have made the heaven, the heaven of heavens, with all their host, the earth and all that is on it, the seas and all that is in them; and you preserve all of them; and the host of heaven worships you" (ESV). Throughout the first chapter of the Bible, we can read about how God precisely placed the Earth in its spot in the universe. He created the sun, moon, stars, galaxies, constellations, and planets. You could even say He double, triple, and quadruple-"spaced"!

When God creates, He creates powerfully and perfectly. He created … *creating*. And, very unlike my pitiful article, when He saw all He had made, He said it was *good*.

What awesome creativity came into play when God made the universe. And when we contemplate God as our awesome Creator, worship can't help but follow. "Worthy are you, our Lord and God, to receive glory and honor and power, for you created all things, and by your will they existed and were created" (Revelation 4:11 ESV).

What a Creator

The Creator of the universe deserves all our worship.

I love the way the Amplified Version of the Bible describes the beginning of creation in John 1:1-2. "In the beginning [before all time] was the Word (Christ), and the Word was with God, and the Word was God Himself. He was [continually existing] in the beginning [co-eternally] with God."

From the very beginning, God had a plan for all of creation, and that plan starts with Jesus. Just one verse later, we read that "All things were made and came into existence through Him; and without Him not even one thing was made that has come into being" (AMP).

In Hebrews, Jesus is described as "the author and perfecter of our faith" (12:2 ASV). Believing, understanding, internalizing that truth changes how we live. I ever-want this Author to be the all-ruling, creative God of me.

Perfect Creator, You are great, and Your creativity is so inspiring. The heavens declare Your greatness, and I can't help but do it, too. You really are worthy of all my praise. Father, create in me a clean heart today as I look to You, the One who made all things. Amen.

27
And the One Who Died for Me

Chantal Hite

"Since he did not spare even his own Son but gave him up for us all, won't he also give us everything else?"

(Romans 8:32 NLT).

"He was handed over to die because of our sins, and he was raised to life to make us right with God"

(Romans 4:25 NLT).

Condemned. Death row. The words pronounced over me were devastating. The heaviness of those words hung in the air. What had I done to get here? How could this awful sentence be reversed? I heard the panic in my voice as it rang through the courtroom. "Your Honor. Please. Hear me out. What have I done to receive such a sentence?"

For as long as I could remember, I had been the model citizen. I worked so hard to earn the love and admiration of those around me. I was obedient, kind, quiet, hardworking—not the type of person who deserved to die. Wasn't that punishment for hardened criminals? People who made a profession out of crimes too heinous to mention?

The Judge looked at me with a sober expression, compassion lacking in his eyes. He repeated my name and asked that the records be summoned and read before the court. As the file was pulled and the bailiff read, the panic rose in my heart. These crimes they spoke of were dating back further than even I could remember. It was as if the court had recorded in their files every word spoken and every action I had ever taken. Not only that, but somehow, they pulled from their files the ugliest parts of me. The side of me I worked so hard to keep hidden even from those closest to me. The part of me I wanted no one to see and wished even I could forget.

I understood at that moment that I was guilty and without excuse. There was nothing I could offer the Judge in my defense. The front that I had so long maintained was shattered. I deserved death.

An Advocate

I lost all desire to fight. Who was I to stand before this Judge who knew the real me so well? He was fair and just in His judgments. Once again, I heard my voice ring through the courtroom, "Your Honor, I'm sorry. You have judged correctly."

At that moment, from the back of the room, a kind, gentle voice interrupted. "Your Honor. As You well know, I am qualified to speak for the accused. I am in good standing with the court, and, if You were to retrieve my record, You would see that it is perfectly clean. Not a crime to report. I would like to beg the court for mercy for the accused."

I stood amazed. Anticipation filled my chest, and my heart beat wildly.

The man continued, "Your Honor. You have judged correctly. The crimes do require death."

My heart dropped, and my hope faded.

"But today," he said, "I offer myself to pay the requirements for the freedom of the accused."

With wild anticipation, I looked at the Judge. Why would this man, about whom I knew so little and to whom I had nothing to offer willingly accept *my* penalty? What would the Judge say? Would I go free? Before I knew it, the man was rushed from the courtroom, condemned to pay the price of the crimes that I deserved.

And me, the chains and cuffs that held me fell to the ground. I was free.

The One who Died for Me

The Bible says, "No one is righteous—not even one" (Romans 3:10 NLT), and "Everyone has sinned; we all fall short of God's glorious standard" (Romans 3:23 NLT). And there is a cost to sin. The cost is death (Romans 6:23). But God, in all His mercy, took my place. He is the One who died for me.

Because of that, He begs and deserves to be the God of me. The God I wake up to, live and breathe for. The God I allow to change the way I think and live. The God who fills my heart with passion and life and love. The God of me gave Himself to set me free and paid the cost for my sins. He took my place. I stood condemned, and He died for me.

Oh beautiful Savior, thank You for dying for me and taking the punishment I deserved. Help me understand the impact of my sins and brokenness. Help me understand the price You paid and the magnitude of Your love. Please

let it change me. Make me into the person You want me to be. Help me not allow sin to control me anymore. I give my life, my thoughts, my words, and my desires to You. I love You.

28

So I Will Lift My Hands and Lift My Soul

Mary Brittan Burgess

"The Amalekites came and attacked the Israelites at Rephidim. Moses said to Joshua, 'Choose some of our men and go out to fight the Amalekites. Tomorrow I will stand on top of the hill with the staff of God in my hands.' So Joshua fought the Amalekites as Moses had ordered, and Moses, Aaron and Hur went to the top of the hill. As long as Moses held up his hands, the Israelites were winning, but whenever he lowered his hands, the Amalekites were winning. When Moses' hands grew tired, they took a stone

and put it under him and he sat on it. Aaron and
Hur held his hands up — one on one side, one on
the other — so that his hands remained steady till
sunset. So Joshua overcame the Amalekite army
with the sword"

(Exodus 17:8-13 NIV).

I will never forget that November day my freshman year of college. I had been at this whole "making new friends" thing for a few months. You know, the friends everyone promises you'll make in college. Those lifelong bridesmaid-in-your-wedding types of friends. But I felt like I wasn't quite getting it right.

I was looking for a friend who believed the same as I did. Someone I could talk to about anything. Someone who understood my deep desire for Christ and who would push me toward Him. Despite going to a Christian college, I wasn't finding that friend. So finally, that November day, I got down on my knees and lifted my hands up to the Lord and begged Him for a friend. It wasn't anything fancy, long, or drawn out. I just simply admitted I could no longer do this on my own, and that I needed the Lord to step in. I prayed for all the things a girl dreams about when she thinks about her lifelong best friend from college.

The Lord must've been just waiting for me to surrender that part of my life to Him, because by the end of the week I had met her. I don't know if there is such a thing as friendship at first sight, or if God was smiling heartily at the situation, but three days later, I met Sarah Beth.

One of our mutual friends, Reed introduced us. He still takes all the credit to this day, by the way. Sarah Beth and I wound up sitting next to each other at dinner before a semi-formal. The rest is history.

Open Your Hands to the Lord

It didn't take me long to see that the Lord had provided in a miraculous way. My parents still tease me and call Sarah Beth my "new best friend," because when I went home for Thanksgiving a week and a half later, I could not stop talking about her. My parents thought it was funny, since they had visited me several times that semester and never heard a word about her.

Our hands say a lot about the posture of our hearts. Not to say that raising your hands is some sort of magical prayer posture that helps your prayer get to the Lord a little more quickly. But sometimes it can say a lot about what's going on inside of us. When our hands are closed to the Lord, it can be symbolic of hearts that still say we can do it ourselves. When we lift our hands up to Him, it's a sign of surrender, understanding that we need the Lord to move in our lives.

Moses models this better than just about anyone in the Bible. In Exodus 17, Joshua, Moses' right-hand man, told Moses their enemies, the Amalekites, were coming to attack. So Moses commanded Joshua to send some of their men out to fight. Moses said he would go to the top of the mountain and lift his hands up to the Lord with the staff of God in his hands. "So Joshua fought the Amalekites as Moses had ordered, and Moses, Aaron, and

Hur went to the top of the hill. As long as Moses held up his hands, the Israelites were winning, but whenever he lowered his hands, the Amalekites were winning" (vv. 10-11 NIV).

How Does a Story from 3,500 Years Ago Apply to Me?

How cool is that? Moses knew the Israelites could not win the battle without the help of the Lord, and the posture of his hands demonstrated exactly that. But it gets better. Thankfully for Moses, the Lord provided him some great friends. "When Moses' hands grew tired, they took a stone and put it under him and he sat on it. Aaron and Hur held his hands up—one on one side, one on the other—so that his hands remained steady till sunset. So Joshua overcame the Amalekite army with the sword" (vv. 12-13 NIV).

I see some great parallels here in Moses winning the battle and my own life experience trying to find a friend. The first is that who your friends are matters. The Lord gave us community for a purpose, so we could be in fellowship with those who draw us closer to Him. It's not that we shouldn't be friends with any non-believers. I am not suggesting we act like the Pharisees. However, there is a special place in our lives for friends who push us to look more like Jesus. Friends who will stand beside us when we want to put our hands down and surrender the battle to the enemy, and who will remind us why fighting Satan is always worth it.

If you feel like a close friend is a piece that's missing from your life, pray for one. Pray that God provides a Sarah Beth in your life.

The second parallel that jumps off the page at me is the posture of Moses' hands as a reflection of his heart. He recognized, understood, and moved forward with action, knowing that the battle was something he needed to give the Lord.

We have all been together on this 30-day journey that is quickly coming to a close. So on day 28, what do you need to entrust to the Lord? What "little g god" do you need to surrender to Him? What do you need to lift your hands and your soul to Him about today? Maybe it's a relationship, an addiction, a desire, or a need. Let's take some time today to get on our hands and knees before the Lord and lift up our hands and souls to Him about whatever He has laid on our hearts.

Father, as I sit here with my hands lifted high, I pray that this posture of my body will reflect the posture of my heart as I come to You. Lord. I confess today that I cannot do this on my own. I need You to intervene in my life. I ask expectantly, Lord, that You would show Your great power in the areas of my life where I find myself powerless. Above all else, all my distractions, all the things I bow down to, all my relationships, any addictions, any other "little g god" I have placed in front of You, Lord, I give to You, recognizing that You are the "God of Me." I surrender all to You today.

29

All I Am, I Give You Control, I Choose You

Kurt Parker

"Many are the plans in the mind of a man, but it is the purpose of the Lord that will stand"

(Proverbs 19:21 ESV).

Let me ask you a question, dear reader. If God were to do the opposite of what you asked Him to do, how would you react? Be honest here. Don't feel like you need to give the churchy answer. Take a second to ponder it. If you asked God for a new job, but stayed stuck in the same one, what would your attitude be? If you desired to live near the beach, but God told you to stay in Middle America, what would you say to Him?

As Christians, we are called to give God control. But isn't it true that when we really dig down and think about giving God control or about surrender, we're wanting God to do what we want Him to do? We want Him to give us the relationship, dream job, money—maybe even the healing of our loved one. And if He doesn't, well, we're let down. We think, *I guess God doesn't care about me.*

I think of Jonah, who preached repentance to the people of Nineveh but, more than anything else, wanted God to destroy them. When God didn't do what Jonah wanted, Jonah grew bitter and angry.

Surrender is a Perspective

Our hearts can often reflect that attitude. It isn't about giving God control, it's about trying to control God. We want God to bend the knee to our will—do things our way—instead of bending our knee to Him. We're trying to switch places with God. We desire control.

In our culture, we often have a warped view of giving God control. When we give God control, we think we're giving Him something He doesn't already have. Surrender isn't giving God control of something we ourselves have control over. It's more of a realization that He has always had control and then trusting Him with all. Surrender is less of an action and more of a perspective.

When the Nazis surrendered during WWII, they didn't do so because they still had power and thought,

Well, we're bored, so might as well give up. No, they were in total defeat! Their surrender was a recognition of that defeat. Likewise, when we surrender to God, we realize we don't have control and we never did. With that understanding we can truly trust God with our lives. God always has the best for us, even if it doesn't look like what we desire.

Joy in the Storm

A few years ago, I was in a terrible car accident. I was stopped on the highway and was rear-ended by a semi-truck going full speed. I was driving a Honda Civic, so it wasn't a fair fight. My car lost the battle, and I almost lost as well.

I vividly remember the drive home from the hospital. It was dark and silent on the winding road to our house. The moon shone through trees barren from the grip of winter. It felt like a dream. I burst into tears at the thought that I was still alive.

Sometimes we think we're immortal, that tragedies can't happen to us. But they can, and they do. In that accident, I remembered how little control I have over anything. I don't control my heartbeat, and I can't control other drivers. God does. I firmly believe God intervened that day and rescued my life. Even the EMTs echoed that belief.

Storms come in this life. Jesus promises us they will. He also has a way to weather those storms when they rear their ugly heads. In Matthew 7:24-27, Jesus tells us that when we listen to His words, we are building our lives on Him as our foundation. When the storms come—and they will—as they beat against the house, our house will stand.

Only by choosing to follow Jesus and putting our trust in Him can we weather the heartache of this life. Trusting in Him means we surrender to Him. The good in this life and the bad, we give everything over to Him. We realize we have no control over the storms, but He does. Anything He does is good, and we trust Him.

In the book of Philippians, we find Paul writing from his prison cell in Rome. Here Paul references "joy" or "rejoicing" sixteen times. *Sixteen times!* Joy in the face of adversity seems to be a common thread through this letter. How could anyone find anything joyful about being in prison? Perspective. Every moment for Paul was a chance to watch God work, a chance to see God move in his life and the lives of those around him. God's will overcomes our circumstances. God stands alone in His greatness. He can move even when it feels like the world is standing still.

Likewise, as we stand in the midst of storms, as we search for answers to the "whys" in our lives, as we wrestle with the ache in our hearts, we can find joy because God is going to make good from it. Paul gives his reason for his joy in verse 13. "I can do all things through Him who strengthens me" (Philippians 4:13 ESV).

Our Strength to Overcome

Jesus is the great overcomer. He is our strength to get through the night. His heart is kind towards us. If we really believe God is who He says He is, why would we ever want control of our lives? His ways are so much better than ours.

The car accident left me with lasting effects on my body and my brain. I wouldn't have chosen to be in that car accident if I had the choice. God has a purpose for my life, He has a purpose for the car accident, and it is all to bring Him glory.

I believe God has a purpose for your life, too. If we surrender to His will, if we build our lives on His Word, then regardless of the storm, we can overcome. We can find joy.

Follow Jesus wherever He leads you. Submit to Him. God's heart is kind toward you. Sometimes we need to see the calm after the storm to see the purpose of it. Jesus' disciples didn't understand His death for days.

Have hope, be steadfast, give your life to God, and watch what He does.

Jesus, I give everything to You. I give You control of my life. I give You my heart, my family, my struggles, my pain, and my questions. Jesus, I know Your heart is kind toward me, and You have demonstrated Your love for me on the cross. I trust You. No matter the storm, I will stand firm in You. Here's my heart, Lord. Take it. I am Yours.

30

Let the Whole World Know You are the God of Me

Rhonda Rhea

"For it is you who light my lamp;
the LORD my God lightens my darkness"

(Psalm 18:28 ESV).

Here's the message I considered texting to everyone I know: *I'm at that décor mega-super-store. It's so mega and so super that I'm pretty sure I've been here for four days. I can no longer feel my feet. Please send help.*

I fought off the urge to send the message, but that shopping trip finally ended like this:

Cashier, as I'm checking out: Did you find everything okay?

Me, unloading my eight carts: Not really but I'm too weary and dehydrated to go on.

Cashier, deadpanning: Do you have a rewards card?

Okay, it probably wasn't four days, and I might not have had eight carts. But there were some deals I could not say no to. It was like, if I stopped shopping, the store would instantly sell out of some piece of prize decor. So I pressed on. Like a total maniac. Like a total maniac with feelingless feet.

Sold Out and Soldiering On

Paul charges us to press on with a better enthusiasm, in a better direction, and for a better purpose. In Philippians 3:14, he says, "I pursue as my goal the prize promised by God's heavenly call in Christ Jesus" (CSB). "Press on" is from the Greek "dioko." It implies a sold-out, soldiering on, lifelong commitment. And it's in the present tense, so that we understand that this pressing on is not just for a couple of hours. Not even for four days. Paul is saying that this pressing on is the constant habit of his life.

Warren Wiersbe said that the Greeks used "dioko" to describe an "intense endeavor," as in "a hunter eagerly pursuing his prey." Yes, that does rather describe my shopping. But so much more, I want it to describe my passion for pursuing Christ. I want this to be the constant habit of my life.

Paul clues us in about what that pursuit looks like just prior. In verse 12 of the same chapter, he says, "Not that I have already reached the goal or am already perfect, but I make every effort to take hold of it." Then he shares his motivation with us. His why. His "because." "Because I also have been taken hold of by Christ Jesus" (CSB).

To be taken hold of by Christ is to be cherished. Cradled. This is the most loving, eternally nurturing hold.

Big G God of Me

Oh, how I want to pursue Him and endeavor to live out His call—out of love for the one who has redeemed me, the one who has taken loving hold of me. The prize? When we pursue this goal—when we recognize Him as the Big G God of me—we win His forever presence. There's nothing in the universe more mega or more super. We're talking about the reward card to end all reward cards.

I'm encouraged as well that Paul wasn't necessarily all about perfection. He freely admitted he was not there. That tells me it's a growth process, and it reminds me I need to be growing and maturing. He says in verse 15, "Therefore, let all of us who are mature think this way" (CSB). The Amplified version expands on it this way: "All of us who are mature [pursuing spiritual perfection] should have this attitude" (Philippians 3:15 AMP).

Press on. Let's do it. Let's take on this charge. Let's put on this attitude. Let's pursue it. Let's pursue *Him.* I want to pursue my Jesus with all the strength I have.

It's a beautiful truth that as we pursue Him with a willing and humble heart, the world takes notice. Jesus said, "You are the light of the world. A city set on a hill cannot be hidden. Nor do people light a lamp and put it under a basket, but on a stand, and it gives light to all in the house. In the same way, let your light shine before others, so that they may see your good works and give glory to your Father who is in heaven" (Matthew 5:14-16 ESV). Every one of us who seeks to surrender, who desires with every part of the heart to give glory to the Father, is shiny. As I crave the closeness of a God who is God of me—God of every part of me—the world can't miss the light, even if they try. It's a shininess that brings glory to the Father in heaven. There's nothing sweeter in this life.

With All I've Got

So yes, I want to pursue Him with everything I've got, make sure He is the God of every part of me, and let God get the glory as the world glimpses His light. I can't think of a thing I wouldn't surrender to see that happen. Everything I've got—even way past all the feeling in my feet.

Father, not a day goes by that I'm not blown away by the glorious thought that I have been taken hold of by Your Son, Christ Jesus. Empower me, I pray, to press on—and to do it in a way that makes a difference in the lives of those around me. Lord, may the whole world see that You are the God of me, and may Your work in me make me shiny for You. I make it my life-long commitment even right now, in Jesus name. Amen.

Conclusion

Jared Prindle

Ancient Greek mythology is such a funny thing. They had an entire hierarchy of gods and goddesses and titans—and let's not forget about good ol' Hercules. But have you ever heard of a "muse"? No, I'm not talking about the 90s rock band. Though, I do like them. Apparently there were nine of these little creatures, "muses," who brought the fun, festivity, music, theatre, and art to Mt. Olympus where the gods lived.

It was believed that if a songwriter wrote a good song, it was because one of the nine muses had visited them and given them the melody. It's actually where we get the word "music." As you can guess, people would do various rituals and gather charms to get one of these muses to show up and bless them with a song or some other creative idea.

Hold that thought in one hand, we'll come back to it.

Thoughts about I AM

Moses was a murderer who fled to Midian, where he took a job as a shepherd (see the book of Exodus). I'm sure he wondered if God was even real, or if He was, if He cared about his situation. But then one day Moses notices a bush that's burning, but isn't burning up. The way the story reads, Moses "turned aside" (Exodus 3:4) from what he was doing to see what was up with the bush that wouldn't die.

Moses encounters God (big G) at this bush. He tells Moses how He's going to use him to rescue the Israelites and establish the nation of Israel, and how he will lead them into the promised land.

"That's amazing!" Moses yells. Well, not exactly. But he asked, "If I come to the people of Israel and say to them, 'The God of your fathers has sent me to you,' and they ask me, 'What is his name?' what shall I say to them?" (Exodus 3:13 ESV).

God answered Moses, "Ehyeh Asher Ehyeh," which means, "I Am who I Am."

Hold that thought in your other hand; we'll come back to it.

Thoughts about the Song

Ever since I was in high school and realized girls love a guy who can write music, I have been writing songs. I started off trying to make them laugh. I wrote funny jingles and songs about the teachers. Then, as I grew a little, I tried to write more serious songs. Fortunately for me, church was the primary venue I had for singing, so most of mine were worship songs, or at least biblically themed.

Over the last 16 years or so, I've been attempting to write good songs. I've probably written over a thousand songs, most of which are in a dump somewhere (rightfully so; they were garbage). I still have a lot to learn, but I have had the pleasure of experiencing songwriting in seasons of drought, where every lyric and chord was a labor of love. And then there are seasons when it's like the lyrics and melody come from somewhere else, and it's difficult to write them down fast enough. It's like you have to catch the ideas on paper quickly or the new ideas will just shove out the previous ones. It's exciting and amazing!

Weaving the Thoughts Together

The ancient Greeks sought after the muses and went through rituals and superstitions to attract their attention, so the muses would bless them with a song or a creative idea. But we see in the story of Moses that God chose a nobody-special-shepherd-murderer. God wanted to be everything to him and wanted to use him to do great things. See the difference?

God continued to do this sort of thing throughout the Bible. Seriously. Look at the lineup of mess-ups. Gideon was a coward. David was an adulterous murderer. Peter was a clueless fisherman. Paul persecuted the church. God came to these people, called them out of their darkness, and became their "muse" and their (big G) God.

So when Matt asked the musical staff for some new worship music for our church, I sat down for a bit of fun songwriting. I had no expectations, other than just writing a simple song God could use to bless our church. Oh yes. And I thought it would be fun to include "life on purpose" (our church's slogan) and "refuge" (the name of our student ministry) in the song.

I remember sitting in Cornerstone Coffee Shop with a little melody in my head, and 30 minutes later the lyrics and melody were pretty much done. I ran home, sat down at the piano, and had the chords and melody ironed out within an hour. It was amazing. It felt like God had directed the words. He was my muse. I'm not claiming to be a prophet. Nor do I think "God of Me" is out of the ordinary in terms of worship music these days. There is currently so much great worship music. But I think it's a song from God for NorthRoad.

And do you want to know my favorite part of the song? The hook line at the end of the chorus, "You are! You are! You are! You are! Oh, You are the God of me."

I know that sounds like a joke, but I'm serious.

Why is that part my favorite? Because it's the actual name of God! It's the name for Himself God told Moses to tell the Israelites. "Ehyeh" means "I am" (or "I will be"), so when the Israelites called upon their God, they used the name, "Yahweh," which means "You are" (or "You will be").

Isn't that so cool? And I can't even take credit for this. I honestly didn't realize it until weeks after we recorded it.

So What's My Point?

Who is God to you? No, not "who do you think God is?" But who is God in relation to you? Is He *really* your God? Is He your everything? Or is He just a nondescript something to make you feel good, but to whom you never really fully commit?

God doesn't want to be one god among many, any more than my wife wants to be one wife among many. My wife wants to be my one and only, and rightfully so. Likewise, God wants to be our one and only. He wants to be our God, our muse, our light, our hope, our peace, our salvation, our confidence, our strength, and so much more. He wants to be our everything.

Will you let Him?

You can hear *God of Me*, the song that inspired this book, free on Spotify at NorthRoad Worship (it's also available at Apple Music).

Get to Know NorthRoad —
And we would love to get to know you, too.

God has called NorthRoad Church to reach out. To reach out to individuals. To reach out to families. To reach out to people in all walks of life, and to love them, meet their needs, and help them find God's amazing purpose for their lives.

It's our desire as a church to be a beacon of hope and a light in a dark world, bringing the tightest focus to the light of Christ, exposing darkness, and brightly shining His love in every way.

NorthRoad Church currently has two campus locations in the St. Louis area. Anytime you're in the neighborhood, you are invited, welcome, accepted, wanted.

Find us at:

NorthRoad Moscow Mills Campus
49 College Campus Drive
Moscow Mills, MO 63362

Livestream at facebook.com/northroadchurch or on YouTube at NorthRoad Community Church

NorthRoad Harvester Campus
1120 Jungs Station Road
St. Charles, MO 63303

Livestream at facebook.com/NorthRoadHarvester

You're also invited to get to know us better at NorthRoadChurch.com

Most importantly, if you have questions about knowing and following Jesus, there's nothing we would love more than chatting with you. Contact our Care Pastor, Richie Rhea, anytime from anywhere at richie@northroad-church.com.

Bible Versions

Scripture quotations marked ESV are taken from The Holy Bible, English Standard Version® (ESV®) Copyright © 2001 by Crossway, a publishing ministry of Good News Publishers. All rights reserved. ESV Text Edition: 2007

Scripture quotations marked (NIV) are taken from the Holy Bible, New International Version®, NIV®. Copyright © 1973, 1978, 1984, 2011 by Biblica, Inc.™ Used by permission of Zondervan. All rights reserved worldwide. www.zondervan.com The "NIV" and "New International Version" are trademarks registered in the United States Patent and Trademark Office by Biblica, Inc.™

Scripture quotations marked AMP are taken from the Amplified® Bible, Copyright © 1954, 1958, 1962, 1964, 1965, 1987 by The Lockman Foundation. Used by permission." (www.Lockman.org)

Scripture quotations marked NLT are taken from the Holy Bible, New Living Translation, copyright ©1996, 2004, 2007 by Tyndale House Foundation. Used by permission of Tyndale House Publishers, Inc., Carol Stream, Illinois 60188. All rights reserved.

Scripture quotations marked CSB have been taken from the Christian Standard Bible®, Copyright © 2017 by Holman Bible Publishers. Used by permission. Christian Standard Bible® and CSB® are federally registered trademarks of Holman Bible Publishers.

Scripture quotations marked (NIrV) are taken from the Holy Bible, New International Reader's Version®, NIrV® Copyright © 1995, 1996, 1998, 2014 by Biblica, Inc.™ Used by permission of Zondervan. All rights reserved worldwide. www.zondervan.comThe "NIrV" and "New International Reader's Version" are trademarks registered in the United States Patent and Trademark Office by Biblica, Inc.™